Nobody asked for my opinion, but (here it is anyway)

second edition

Jack D'Aurora

ISBN:

9 781667 191249

Dedication

As with the first edition, this book is dedicated to my father, Anthony C. D'Aurora (1914 to 2001). Though he was born of humble Italian immigrant parents, Pop's grammar was flawless, and his writing was elegant.

Table of Contents

Acknowledgments

My wife, Debbie, reads every op-ed I draft before I submit it for publication. She's my personal quality control check and an invaluable source of assistance.

My daughter, Allison, helped with the book's formatting. She likes this book very much because, she says, when she reads it to her one-year old son, Vinny, he falls asleep right away.

Introduction

This book is a collection of everything of mine that has been published since 2013. A frequent theme with my writing is social justice, a subject that doesn't get enough press.

Death Penalty

Save millions by killing Ohio's death penalty
May 9, 2013, Columbus Business First

How many Ohio businesses run their operations with little regard for the expenditure of time and money? Ohio ignores both every time it sends an inmate to death row.

Richard Beasley, the so-called Craigslist killer, was sentenced to death on April 4, 2013, for murdering three men. Based on the average stay on death row for Ohio inmates, if Beasley is executed, his execution date could be as far off as November of 2032. Gauging from his physical appearance, he may die of natural causes before he is executed, and that would be a blessing for Ohio in terms of time and money.

In addition to appealing purported trial court errors, death row inmates pursue post-conviction proceedings before the Ohio Supreme Court and *habeas corpus* proceedings before the U.S. District Court. These post-conviction and *habeas* proceedings focus on procedural issues and consume years on end. All of this is required to ensure due process, but it's expensive.

An army of personnel is required to execute an inmate. In each case, the state is initially represented by two attorneys from the county prosecutor's office and later by two attorneys from the attorney general's office. Inmates are represented by two attorneys, whose fees were likely paid by the county, state or federal government, depending on the proceeding. To this group we add state trial court judges, Ohio Supreme Court justices, federal district court and appellate court judges, staff attorneys and other support staff for all these judges, county sheriffs, expert witnesses, parole board members (for clemency hearings) and Ohio Department of Corrections personnel. Before you know it, millions of dollars are spent annually to execute killers.

Alternatively, we could repeal the death penalty and award life sentences without the possibility of parole. The legal proceedings would end about two years after trial, and, even when factoring in the cost of incarceration, total savings would easily be tens of millions of dollars annually. Families of victims would also have closure much sooner. As it stands, closure is dependent on a seemingly never ending and bewildering series of legal proceedings.

In April 2012, Connecticut joined 16 other states and the District of Columbia by abolishing the death penalty. Cost was an issue. The *Huffington Post* reported that repealing the death penalty is expected to save the state $850,000 a year in the next two years and $5 million in subsequent years, presumably after the few remaining death row inmates are executed.

On May 3, Maryland abolished the death penalty. A 2008 study by the Urban Institute concluded that a death penalty case costs Maryland approximately $1.9 million more than a non-death penalty case.

Maryland has only five inmates on death row, and Connecticut has 11. The expenses of capital punishment for these states pale in comparison to Ohio, where we have 141 inmates on death row. If we were to study the cost, it would likely be jaw-dropping.

Yet capital punishment continues because it satisfies our need for retribution. Believing that killers should be eliminated is reassuring in a violent world.

Still, how many citizens would advocate death if they knew the real cost? Most people have no idea what the death penalty costs us; based on talks with several state representatives, this includes most elected officials in the General Assembly. The problem is that the total costs of execution are hidden, not purposefully, but because they are not segregated in separate line items in county and state budgets.

A federal appellate judge said it well: "[T]he choice to pay for the death penalty is a choice *not* to pay for other public goods like roads, schools, parks, public works."

**Death penalty is ineffective,
costs too much time and money**
December 23, 2018, The Columbus Dispatch

What message will Ohio send if it seeks the death penalty for the four members of the Wagner family accused of murdering eight members of the Rhoden family in Pike County in 2016? That the death penalty is the only way justice can be served for such brutal killings? That executing the Wagners is a necessary deterrent? That Ohio is tough on crime?

The answer is, all of above, but Ohio will also be demonstrating it prefers the charade of capital punishment over confronting the reality that it's a profligate use of time and money.

To support capital punishment, you have to ignore the disconnect between meting out a death sentence and then waiting 20 years before the execution happens. You have to disregard the tremendous expense that comes with capital punishment. Worse yet, you have to be blind to the lunacy of repeatedly trying cases and obtaining convictions, only so that you can waste time and money in years of post-trial proceedings.

We have 138 offenders on Ohio's Death Row. Twenty-one have been there for at least 15 years, another 46 for at least 20 years, and another 21 for at least 30 years. If the Wagners are found guilty and given the death penalty, perhaps two years will pass before the Ohio Supreme Court issues a decision on their direct appeals to the court. Then another 15 to 20 years will pass as they pursue post-trial proceedings in federal court, where every inch of their cases will be reviewed for a variety of issues.

None of this comes cheap. Before Maryland abolished capital punishment, the average capital-eligible case resulting in a death sentence cost the state $1.9 million more than a murder case where the death penalty was not sought. It's estimated New Jersey saves $2.6 million annually by having abolished capital punishment. Were North Carolina to follow suit, it would save approximately $10.8 million annually. The cost in Ohio? Good question.

The added expense comes with longer trials and all the resources—lawyers, judges, court staff, law enforcement personnel, correctional personnel—that go into the post-trial review proceedings.

Besides being costly, the U.S. Department of Justice finds there is no evidence capital punishment deters crime.

Why not curtail that post-trial procedure? Because doing so likely creates constitutional law problems, but more importantly, it raises the likelihood of executing the wrong people. I've met men who were wrongly convicted and lived on Ohio's Death Row for years before being exonerated.

But still, we press on with the death penalty. Because executing murderers satisfies some dark need within us for revenge. Because politicians like to crow about being tough on crime, and nothing says toughness like an execution. Because murderers deserve death. Because you can't put a price on justice.

But cost matters everywhere else in life. If capital punishment were judged on a cost-effective basis, it would serve as a case study in business schools for how not to run a company. Where are the conservative spending hawks when it comes to capital punishment?

Intelligent people perpetuate the myth that capital punishment serves a purpose, as if it won't involve an inordinate amount of time and money. It's akin to repeatedly hitting yourself on the head with a mallet and hoping it won't hurt the next time.

If we repeal capital punishment, we can still adequately punish murderers and safeguard the community by making a life sentence without parole—as in, once in jail, you never leave—the ultimate sentence for all murders. After a murderer's state court appeal is exhausted, he would no longer be part of our world.

There would be finality—all in about two years. The victim's family would know with certainty the murderer will die in prison. And the state of Ohio would be saving millions of dollars.

So why do we keep hitting ourselves with that mallet?

Criminal justice system prioritizes procedure over results
December 17, 2019, The Columbus Dispatch

Gov. Mike DeWine has put a hold on executions. He's bothered that the drug protocol used by the state to execute inmates causes severe pain and mimics waterboarding. DeWine is right to be bothered, but more than anything, he should be concerned for how flawed the system is.

The Death Penalty Information Center tells us that 163 Death Row inmates nationwide, including nine Ohioans, have been exonerated since 1973. Seven of those Ohioans were exonerated in the last 16 years. It's impossible to tell how many innocent inmates have been executed.

Which leads to the next point: the judicial system places priority on procedure over outcome. So long as you have had a trial that meets the requirements of Due Process, the result doesn't matter.

Justices Antonin Scalia and Clarence Thomas have told us the U.S. Constitution guarantees certain rights but not correct verdicts: "This Court has never held that the Constitution forbids the execution of a convicted defendant who has had a full and fair trial but is later able to convince a habeas court that he is 'actually' innocent." The court has expressed "considerable doubt that any claim based on alleged 'actual innocence' is constitutionally cognizable."

From a technical point of view, Scalia and Thomas might be correct, and that's the problem. Where an inmate sought review of his case based on claims of innocence, the key issue to Justices Sandra J. O'Connor and Anthony M. Kennedy was "whether a fairly convicted and therefore legally guilty person is constitutionally entitled to yet another judicial proceeding in which to adjudicate his guilt anew, 10 years after conviction, notwithstanding his failure to demonstrate that constitutional error infected his trial."

Though the facts presented by the inmate may not have been that strong, what's troubling is that O'Connor and Kennedy referred to the nation's "high degree of confidence in its criminal trials," which is attributed, "in no small part because the Constitution offers unparalleled protections against convicting the innocent."

But the system does convict the innocent.

And the poorer you are and less able to afford competent counsel, the greater the likelihood of error and wrongful conviction.

We have tried to insulate ourselves from the brutality of executions while satisfying our appetite for killing offenders, and so we have endeavored to make executions more civilized. The method of killing has evolved from hanging to firing squads to the electric chair to the gas chamber and now lethal injection. As Alex Kozinski, a former federal court appellate judge, puts it, "If we as a society want to carry out executions, we should be willing to face the fact that the state is committing a horrendous brutality on our behalf."

Kozinski, a death penalty proponent, views lethal injection as sugar coating the process. He advocates a return to firing squads. "Sure, firing squads can be messy, but if we are willing to carry out executions, we should not shield ourselves from the reality that we are shedding human blood. If we, as a society, cannot stomach the splatter from an execution ... then we shouldn't be carrying out executions at all."

Which brings us to just how clinical the death system has become. Everyone who has a role in executing the offender—judges, prosecutors, governors—does so at a great distance. It is the difference between dropping bombs from 35,000 and shooting an enemy soldier in close-in combat. The bomber pilot knows on some intellectual level he has killed; the soldier has felt death up close.

No wonder Kozinski admitted, "I'd never want to witness an execution" and then questioned, "whether those of us who make life-and-death decisions on a regular basis should not be required to watch as the machinery of death grinds up a human being. I ponder what it says about me that I can, with cool precision, cast votes and write opinions that seal another human being's fate but lack the courage to witness the consequences of my actions."

Inequities in the Economy

The Texas Coalition for Affordable Power reported in December 2012 that as of the prior June, the average residential electricity price in deregulated states was 13.6 cents per kilowatt hour, compared to 11.7 cents in regulated states. From 2002 to 2010, consumers with deregulated providers paid an average of $3100 more than consumers with regulated providers.

According to an August 2012 survey, the rates for consumers in regulated San Antonio were lower than the rates offered by 16 of the 18 providers that serve unregulated Houston. The city of San Antonio's website states that the average CEO pay for major Texas unregulated providers grew from $2.7 million in 2000 to $7.5 million in 2011 and that "deregulation has had the unintended consequence of discouraging the building of new power plants."

Ohio has also been moving toward telecommunication deregulation. Senate Bill 271, which died in the House last December, would have allowed phone companies to discontinue mandated basic phone service or charge unregulated prices, so long as at least two other companies offered some service at a single point within each of their exchanges (the area covered by the first three numbers of a phone number). The bill did not require that alternatives be available for all or that the alternatives be competitive in price.

The OCC warned that Senate Bill 271 would have forced basic service consumers to switch to more expensive services and pay for unwanted add-ons, and enabled providers to drop service in less profitable areas. According to the Ohio Association of Area Agencies on Aging, nearly all 3000 low income seniors in 10 southeast Ohio counties who earned less than $2130 per month and received state funded home health care used land lines. More expensive cell phone service was likely not a real option for these folks.

Now, because of resistance encountered here and in other states, Maskovyak senses the industry will approach deregulation on a national basis. "I'm hearing the telecoms are headed to the Federal Communications Commission."

"The free market system works well in most respects," said Smalz, "but not when consumers have to purchase necessities like electricity in a complex market with myriad confusing options and minimal consumer protections."

Plan needed to curb high-interest loans
November 24, 2013, The Columbus Dispatch

The Ohio Supreme Court will soon hear a case concerning the Short-Term Loan Act. While the case is important, the bigger issue is how lenders have devised ways to work around the act in making short term, high interest loans known as payday loans.

Passed in 2008, the act eliminated then-existing interest rates of five percent per month for payday loans, limited interest to 28 percent annually and fees to $20, and prohibited lenders from taking a security interest. A subsequent referendum provided that "all short term lenders, including check cashing lenders, would be subject" to the new act.

Lenders, however, never applied for licenses under the act and instead apply for licenses under the Small Loan and Second Mortgage Acts, which permit higher fees. The strategy worked until payday lender Cashland sued a borrower. Though it claimed it had made a "payday" style loan, Cashland was licensed under the Second Mortgage Act, not the Short-Term Loan Act.

The court held that Cashland was not authorized to make the loan and disallowed the interest and fees Cashland claimed. After the decision was affirmed on appeal, Cashland appealed to the Ohio Supreme Court, where the case will be heard on Dec. 10.

Much is at stake. A court brief filed on behalf of Richard F. Keck, former Deputy Superintendent for the Ohio Division of Financial Institutions, stated that upholding the appellate court's decision will "put billions of dollars of loans at risk." Overturning the decision will mean the legislature's effort to regulate payday lending accomplished nothing.

Lenders work around the Short-Term Loan Act by operating under the Small Loan and Second Mortgage Acts. In addition to higher fees, these laws permit loans to be collateralized, and so lenders are now making high interest loans secured by auto titles. According to the Center for Responsible Lending, underwriting these loans is usually limited to a valuation of the borrower's car. Credit checks are generally not required. LoanMax advertises that it "does not use credit scores ... With us, your vehicle is your credit!"

Often unable to repay their loans, borrowers will repeatedly refinance their loans and find themselves on a "long-term debt treadmill." Eugene R. King, Director of the Ohio Poverty Law Center, stated, "A 2013 study found that desperation and lack of options drive people to use payday loans. Only about 14% of borrowers have sufficient income to repay these loans on time."

Not so, said Patrick Crowley, spokesman for the Ohio Consumer Lenders Association.
"Our lenders work with customers to help them repay their loans and stress a higher level of customer service

to help ensure a comprehensive understanding of our financial services and payment options."

Lenders also avoid the Short-Term Loan Act by registering as credit service organizations. By statute, CSOs are limited to assisting with credit issues and obtaining credit but may not act as lenders. CSOs arrange for and administer high interest loans funded by other lenders and charge additional fees. According to Linda Cook, senior attorney for the law center, a borrower's contact is limited to the CSO.

Policy Matters Ohio reported that CSOs usually charge a 25 percent broker fee, while the third-party lenders charge interest of 25 percent and fees. A CSO $500 auto title loan would typically cost $161 in fees and interest and be due in 30 days.

"We need to stop buying the industry's constant argument that payday loans are only for temporary emergencies," stated King. "If we want to promote self-sufficiency for all Ohio families, we need to get serious about controlling predatory small loans."

Crowley sees things differently. "There will always be critics of new financial products. In our mind, customer demand is the ultimate determinant for establishing the worth and viability of a product. Without demand, a product would not exist very long. The laws of economics and behavior determine the success and value of a product."

Short term loans are also made by pawn brokers, who may be getting an income boost. House Bill 192 proposes to reduce the current five percent per month interest rate to three percent but also provides for an additional monthly fee of ten percent of the value of the loan to cover various expenses. So, while a $500 loan under the current loan would cost $25 per month, the monthly cost under H.B. 192, would be $65.

If the legislature genuinely wants to control high interest loans, then it has to come up with a more comprehensive game plan. Right now, we have a patchwork of inconsistent laws.

No gets the poor nowhere
April 10, 2015, Columbus Business First

I'm starting to take stock of how often we hear the word "no" from legislators. Besides being used too frequently, "no" is seldom followed by an effort to find a better alternative.

Congress has said no to raising the minimum wage. Congress is saying no to keeping Medicaid reimbursements at $70 per office visit, opting to let the rate fall back to $40, surely a disincentive to treating the 59 million people enrolled in Medicaid. And many states (but not Ohio) have said no to expanding Medicaid coverage to families of four with annual incomes of 133 percent of the federal poverty level, which for 2015 is $32,252. In 2013, the U.S. Census Bureau put the official poverty rate at 14.5 percent.

What's troubling is that legislators, who have the benefit of taxpayer funded medical coverage and steady employment, find it easy to say no to those who struggle. All the while, the economic gap increases.

An Ohio economic study published by Fortune magazine last October showed that "the wealthiest 160,000 families own as much wealth as the poorest 145 million families." Should this be a concern? The study contends that "there's plenty of evidence that shows that extreme levels of inequality is bad for business ... Unless your business caters to the richest of the rich, opportunities for real growth are scarce."

Nick Hanauer, a "proud and unapologetic capitalist" and "plutocrat," gave a TED talk about the problems with the growing income inequality. To Hanauer, the gap shows that capitalism is not as effective as it should be. If the working poor cannot afford to participate in the economy, the system as a whole suffers. On the other hand, when prosperity increases across the board, then demand increases, and greater production follows, which helps propel the whole economy.

Hanauer wants to see radical change, like increasing significantly the minimum wage. For that reason and others, Forbes magazine thinks his ideas are "near insane." I can't say one way or another; I'm not an economist, but I like how Hanauer is willing to venture far from established thought. Only by doing so do we achieve change.

With every "no," the status quo becomes an even more impenetrable fortress. The premises upon which the status quo is based become unquestionable truths. We hear this when the naysayers reject raising the minimum wage and argue that, as employment becomes more expensive, there will be less of it. Maybe, but as Hanauer points out, Seattle raised its minimum wage to $15 an hour, and continues to prosper (despite questionable goal-line play calling in the last Super Bowl).

Perhaps I shouldn't be so hard on legislators. Think for a moment about how often you hear "no" in your own business or other groups where you belong. Proposals for change are generally met with no. No is reflexive. No is easy. It maintains the status quo, which may not be that good, but the status quo is safe.

Propose change, and you can expect to hear, "We can't do that because," or "We've never done it that way," etc. Rather than pondering whether change is needed or what propels someone to propose change, the first response will almost invariably be an array of insurmountable road blocks or just a flat no.

Maybe raising the minimum wage and increasing medical coverage for the poor are not good ideas. Then what's the answer for a sector of society that lags behind? Saying no to poverty issues without delving deeper into those issues leaves a hole in the economy.

Maybe Hanauer is nuts, but no doesn't lead to change.

The Consumer Finance Protection Bureau stands up for consumers
January 6, 2017, The Columbus Dispatch

Some conservatives sure don't like the Consumer Financial Protection Bureau. President Donald Trump called it "a total disaster." Office of Management and Budget Director Mick Mulvaney, who just succeeded Richard Cordray as the CFPB director, referred to it as "a joke." Columnist Jay Ambrose said the CFPB operates without oversight.

Why are these men upset? Because the CFPB has had the temerity to hold financial institutions accountable.

Before explaining what I mean, let's look at Ambrose's criticism. The CFPB has not been running loose. Twice annually, its director must appear before three Congressional committees, and the CFPB must issue reports. Those reports are to include nine subjects, ranging from problems faced by consumers in obtaining financial services to significant rules issued and enforcement actions taken by the CFPB.

The U.S. Comptroller General is required annually to audit CFPB financial statements and conduct a study of several subjects, such as the impact of regulation "on the safety and soundness" of regulated businesses, and the cost of compliance.

To understand why Trump, Mulvaney and Ambrose don't like the CFPB, pay attention to the two words they didn't say: consumer protection. The CFPB exists to protect consumers, and that necessarily means challenging financial institutions. In the world of the political right, financial institutions are good, and anything that lowers their bottom line—like consumer lawsuits over unfair business practices—is bad.

What has the CPFB been doing that is so terrible? Last October, it sued two companies operating under the name "FDAA" for falsely presenting themselves as affiliates of the federal government. The FDAA used direct mailers that looked like they came from the federal government and deceived consumers into believing that, in exchange for a fee, their debts could be eliminated.

The CFPB fined Wells Fargo Bank $100 million in 2016 for secretly opening more than two million deposit and credit card accounts without authorization. Employees would transfer funds from authorized accounts to temporarily fund the new, unauthorized accounts. This allowed employees to earn additional compensation, while customers were sometimes charged overdraft fees because their original accounts suddenly had insufficient funds.

The tipping point was the CFPB's decision last summer to invalidate arbitration provisions—which are generally forced on consumers—that also preclude consumers from participating in class action suits. Take a look at your own credit card agreements—you're probably obligated to arbitrate disputes and barred from class action lawsuits. You didn't know? Too bad.

The U.S. Chamber of Commerce and several financial associations filed suit in federal court late September, asserting that, because the CFPB is "unconstitutionally structured," the rule had to be vacated. In other words, they filed suit to prevent consumers from filing suit. How's that for irony?

Just over a month later, Trump signed a bill that repealed the rule. Executives from financial institutions breathed a sigh of relief and talked about how arbitration is a good thing for consumers—it's usually not—and then did what business executives generally do: they criticized trial lawyers.

"Arbitration is a well-established and tested process that offers better results for consumers and helps avoid frivolous class-action suits," said Independent Community Bankers of America President Camden Fine. According to Richard Hunt, Consumer Bankers Association president and CEO, the real beneficiary of the rule were "trial lawyers and their wallets."

Maybe there were problems with how the CFPB was structured and perhaps there were other problems as well, but who else was looking out for how consumers were treated? No one.

Ours is a paternalistic system. Those at the top are deemed to know what's best for the country and anything that challenges their position is bad. With Mulvaney now running the CFPB, order has been restored for financial institutions. So sad.

Lawmakers give a pass to corporate welfare
January 31, 2018, The Columbus Dispatch

Just a few weeks before the Tax Cuts and Jobs Act was signed into law last December, Speaker of the House Paul Ryan (R-Wis.) announced it was time to reduce the deficit by cutting entitlements. On talk radio, he said, "We're going to have to get back next year at entitlement reform … it's the health care entitlements that are the big drivers of our debt …"

Ryan is not alone. The Washington Post reported that Sen. Marco Rubio (R-Fla.) stated, "The driver of our debt is the structure of Social Security and Medicare for future beneficiaries." Senator Orrin G. Hatch (R-Utah) refers to these expenditures as "liberal programs" for the poor and a waste of money.

But these lawmakers don't say a word about corporate welfare. The non-partisan research group, Good Jobs First, tracks both federal and state corporate welfare made in the way of grants, allocated tax credits— separate and apart from tax breaks provided in the IRS code—loans and loan guarantees. Lots of big handouts go to big business.

From 2000 to 2017, the federal government alone awarded big business $72.3 billion in grants and allocated tax credits. According to Good Jobs First research director Philip Mattera, federal grants and allocated tax credits are now roughly $10 billion per year, and loans and loan guarantees are $30 billion.

Spanish energy company, Iberdrola, tops the list for federal subsidies received since 2000 at $2.1 billion. NextEra Energy is number two at $1.9 billion.

The logic behind these give-aways is they help corporations create jobs, and that's good for everybody. Still, don't we pride ourselves as a nation that thrives on capitalism and independence? Legislators see otherwise when it comes to big business.

Surprisingly, you don't have to be a good corporate citizen to qualify for corporate welfare. From 1997 through 2015, Goldman Sachs received $675 million in state and local subsidies such as allocated tax credits and property tax abatements. During roughly the same period, Morgan Stanley received $368 million in state and local subsidies. Goldman then paid $5.1 billion to settle a federal action for its role in causing the Great Recession, and Morgan Stanley paid $3.2 billion for its role.

A number of companies on the dole don't pay their employees an adequate wage. The top five Ohio companies in 2017 with the most employees receiving Supplemental Nutrition Assistance Program (SNAP), formerly known as food stamps, are Walmart, McDonald's, Kroger, Bob Evans and Wendy's. Each has received subsidies from Ohio or the federal government or both.

To qualify for SNAP, the maximum monthly income for a family of four is $2632. A total of 11,560 Ohio

Walmart full and part-time employees and family members received SNAP benefits in 2017. For McDonalds employees and family members, the number was 9927. For Kroger, it was 5051. Public records don't identify the employers for Ohioans receiving Medicaid, but the income limitations for Medicaid and SNAP are roughly the same, and so it's likely some Ohio SNAP enrollees also receive Medicaid.

Let's think about this for a minute. Federal and state governments subsidize large corporations, a practice that doesn't get questioned. But some corporations that receive government subsidies pay such low salaries their employees depend on government assistance, which conservatives want to cut.

Why such different attitudes for corporate subsidies and social welfare entitlements? Conservatives work from the premise that the common good flows from the top down. President Donald Trump boasted on Twitter, "TAX CUTS will increase investment in the American economy and in U.S. workers, leading to higher growth, higher wages, and more JOBS!"

But here's the problem: As of as the Census Bureau's 2016 report, we have over 40 million people living in poverty—that's $24,600 in annual income for a family of four. Sure, the trickle down from the tax cut may help, but it won't solve the problem.

And yes, corporate welfare is a drop in the bucket compared to Social Security and other safety net programs, which account for roughly 60 percent of the federal budget. Cutting these programs, however, without remedying the root causes of poverty only further imperils the poor and elderly.

The size of the safety net is just one reason it's such a big target and corporate welfare isn't. There's another as well. Let's follow the money. Good Jobs First reports that 75% of government subsidies go to 965 corporations. NextEra Energy, Southern Company, General Motors and General Electric are in the top 20 for federal grants and allocated tax credits, and according to OpenSecrets.org, collectively spent nearly $33.6 million on federal lobbying in 2017.

Take a guess how much people receiving SNAP and Medicaid spent on lobbying.

U.S. wage gap is not likely to improve
September 25, 2018, Columbus Dispatch

The Pew Research Center reports that income inequality is at its highest point since 1928. Will it ever substantially improve? Not without a dramatic paradigm shift.

From 1979 to 2015, annual wages increased for the bottom 90 percent of Americans by 21 percent, according to the Economic Policy Institute. For the top 1.0 percent, the increase was 105 percent. For the top 0.1 percent, it was 339 percent.

Our system is based on the paradigm, as Professor Scott R. Sanders of Indiana University explains, of financial wealth being the highest good, with any constraint on the pursuit of money being bad. This means that "government regulation of business, industry, agriculture or commercial production and services must be resisted as an infringement on the free market." The corollary is, what's good for those at the top is good for the nation.

The paradigm manifests in several ways, starting with last year's Tax Cut and Jobs Act. The Tax Policy Center calculated that the largest tax cuts as a share of income go to taxpayers in the top 95th to 99th percentiles of income.

Both President Donald Trump and White House Budget Director Mick Mulvaney loathe the Consumer Finance Protection Bureau. After all, this is an agency, according to its website, "that makes sure banks, lenders, and other financial companies treat you (read consumers) fairly" and touts that it has recovered "$12.4 billion in relief for consumers."

The same paradigm influences the justice system. Ohio passed legislation in 2004 that significantly limits damage awards in personal injury cases. The reasoning behind the bill was that "our tort system has caused bankruptcies, loss of jobs, and stifles innovation" and that Ohio businesses were falling further behind. No statistics were presented, and no consideration was given to how the bill would affect people who are injured by someone else's negligence. The bill was promoted as being a "balanced plan," even though it considered only the business community.

The debate over whether we should raise the minimum wage to $15 an hour always gets swallowed by concern for what bad things might follow. Of course, the decisions makers make good salaries, but what about the married breadwinner with two kids who earns just $12 an hour? If we made it a priority to improve his plight and that of the 43 million American who live at the poverty level ($24,339 annual income for a family of four), the discussion would be much different.

Instead of allowing the fear of consequences to determine what we should do, we would be analyzing how to raise wages while concurrently mitigating any negative effects.

But the wage gap is just one part of the problem. A larger one is looming. The loss of jobs due to technological advances poses to be an even larger threat to the financial well-being of many Americans. MIT academics Erik Brynjolfsson and Andrew McAfee believe that technology is starting to destroy jobs faster than it creates them.

Job prospects are diminishing not only in manufacturing, clerical, and retail work but in the professional sector as well. We are starting to witness what Brynjolfsson and McAfee call the "great decoupling" –economic growth with no parallel increase in job creation.

Think about it. Bank tellers are becoming a vanishing breed. Amazon fills your orders with robots. You don't need a sales clerk to buy clothes; a click of your computer mouse will do it. Between automation and globalization, the U.S. has lost millions of manufacturing jobs. My legal profession isn't safe; research doesn't require the same effort it required not many years ago. Soon we will have self-driving trucks.

If workers at the low end of the economic ladder are falling behind now, the problem will only get worse and for more people when more jobs start to disappear. And worse yet, the speed of change is increasing dramatically.

It doesn't seem the people at the top care. But they'll have to at some point.

The economic boom hasn't benefitted everyone
April 29, 2019, The Columbus Dispatch

The Dow Jones has been on the rise, and the unemployment rate is 3.8 percent. The economy is humming, but is everyone benefitting? It depends on where you stand on the economic ladder. Let's take a look, starting at the top.

Wealth at the top is increasing. According to the Spectrum Group, the number of households with a net worth of $1 million to $5 million, not including primary residence, grew in 2016 to 10.8 million; households with a net worth of $100,000 to $1 million increased to 30.5 million.

Those at the top own a larger share of the nation's wealth than in years past. Bloomberg News reported that the top 10 percent's share of the nation's wealth increased from 61 percent in 1989 to 70 percent in 2018, while the bottom 50 percent's share decreased from 3.8 percent to 1.2 percent.

Pew Research Center data shows that, while median income for upper, middle and lower-income households all decreased from 2000 to 2010, median income in 2016 for upper-income households exceeded the 2000 level. Not so for the other groups. For middle-income households, 2016 was roughly the same as 2000; for lower-income households, median income in 2016 was less than in 2000.

No surprise, we have a widening income gap. In 1970, those near the top of the income ladder had 6.9 times as much income as those near the bottom. That ratio increased to 8.7 in 2016, meaning average incomes of $109,578 versus $12,523. And, yes, these numbers are adjusted for inflation.

Despite the economic boom, the poverty picture hasn't changed much. The poverty rate in 2017, 12.3 percent for families—$25,465 annual income for two adults and two children—is roughly what it was in 2007. The same goes for the poverty rate of 18 percent for children under 18 years of age.

What does all this mean in terms of daily living? Advocacy group Prosperity Now tells us several things. Over 20 percent of jobs pay a wage that is below the poverty threshold for a family of four. One in five households experience moderate to significant income fluctuations monthly. Forty percent of households don't have enough savings to make ends meet at the poverty level for three months if their income is interrupted.

Based on a CBS survey conducted last January, the vast majority of workers live paycheck to paycheck. After a 16-day government shutdown in 2013, roughly two-thirds of furloughed federal employees said they had less than two weeks of savings. On the day before payday, one in five reported they had less than a day's pay left in the bank.

The Economic Innovation Group estimates that 50 million Americans live in economically distressed communities, characterized by, on the average: 21.9 percent of adults without a high school degree, a 26.3 percent poverty rate, a 14.7 percent housing vacancy rate, median income that is 68.2 percent of the nation's median income, and net job losses.

Most of these communities have been on a downward trajectory for years and are unable to attract new business, and so they continue to fall further behind. The Tax Cuts and Job Act of 2017 creates incentives that will supposedly spur investment in these areas.

Demand at food pantries and evictions evidence how a large sector of the population suffers. When the Mid-Ohio Food Bank opened in 1980, it distributed 240,000 meals per year. It now distributes enough food to make 140,000 meals each day, yet hunger persists.

Over 700,000 Ohio tenant households spend more than 30 percent of their income on housing, and one-fourth spend over half, according to the Ohio Housing Finance Agency. The gap between income and rent resulted in18,000 eviction actions last year in Franklin County.

But there's some good news: the large majority our national leaders are comfortable. OpenSecrets.org tells us that in 2015 70 senators were millionaires and the median net worth of representatives increased to $875,000.

Eliminating poverty requires new paradigm, mindset
June 7, 2019, The Columbus Dispatch

Is the nation's and Ohio's poverty rate an inescapable
fact of life or one we choose to ignore? The breadth of
the problem is inescapable: 16.7 percent of Franklin
County residents live at the poverty level—$25,100
annual income for a family of four—and the poverty rate
has increased in every large Ohio city from 1999 to the
2013-2017 period. At last count, it's 20.8 percent in
Columbus and 36.8 percent in Youngstown.

If we want to fix the problem, there are plenty of things
we can do: increase jobs through government investment
in infrastructure, raise the minimum wage, invest in
childcare, and countless other things. Coming up with
ideas is easy. The challenge is with mustering the
political will to execute those ideas. Doing so requires
two fundamental changes.

First, let's change our focus. We operate under the
paradigm that what is good for those at the top of the
economy is good for everyone else. It's a top-down
approach, and while it has some merit, the lion's share of
the benefit from government economic planning favors
those at the top. Not nearly enough benefit finds its way
to those at the lower rungs of the economic ladder. We
need solutions that directly benefit those at the bottom.

Second, let's disabuse ourselves of the notion that the
poor are indolent and have chosen their lot in life. Sure,
some have made bad choices—who hasn't?—but

poverty is rooted in lack of education, few opportunities and social barriers. Show me a family living in poverty, and I'll show you several prior generations that lived in poverty. Poverty gets passed on because of a lack of hope and opportunity, an absence of positive models, and a fatalistic resignation that life will not get better.

As complicated as the problem is, resolving poverty comes down to three steps. The first is to make its elimination a priority. If we can put a man on the moon, we can end poverty, and ending poverty will require the same level of concerted effort.

Second, study the problem. Poverty is no different than any other problem. It has its own unique set of factors that create and perpetuate it. Rather than study those factors, conservatives embrace the idea they can help the poor raise themselves up by cutting the social safety net—an idea not backed by science. Until we understand as much about poverty as we did about various diseases we eliminated, poverty will not vanish.

We can gain some insight to the problem by looking at authors J.D. Vance ("Hillbilly Elegy") and Tara Westover ("Educated"). Each grew up in poverty and dysfunctional families, but they beat the odds and went on to postgraduate education and successful careers. Despite their dismal circumstances, each sensed there was more to life than what they were experiencing at home. Let's learn how to help others replicate their success.

Third, politicians have to muster the courage to take on the issue. Working to eliminate poverty means helping those who can offer nothing in return to politicians. That is, the poor don't make political contributions. And offering a path upward for the poor means standing up to significant pressure from interest groups and conservatives whose focus is cutting the social safety net.

We regularly invest in the top of the economic ladder because doing so is believed to increase opportunity overall. In 2015, property-tax abatements of $300 million were awarded to developers in Franklin County. Last year, CoverMyMeds received $85 million in property tax abatements and income tax incentives because it promised to hire more than 1,000 new employees after moving from its current location to Franklinton.

What if the Franklin County commissioners and the city of Columbus made a similar investment in reducing poverty? What type of economic impact might that have in terms of reducing the need for and, thus, the costs associated with the social safety net and the increased buying power those rising up might have?

COVID-19 disproportionately affects low wage earners

August 10, 2020, The Columbus Dispatch

The COVID-19 pandemic has brought to light a problem we refuse to resolve—too many Americans being paid too low a wage—and illustrates a lack of concern for Americans at the bottom of the economic ladder.

Let's look at the numbers. More than 53 million people—44% of all workers aged 18-64—earn median hourly wages of $10.22 and median annual earnings of $17,950, according to research from Brookings. Nearly two-thirds of these people are in their prime working years of 25-54, and 40 percent are raising children. Nearly half are concentrated in 10 occupation groups, such as retail sales, janitorial and pest control, and personal care.

Workers in essential businesses must continue to work for low wages while putting themselves at greater risk of infection. They toil because they have little choice. Regardless of the health risk—they don't have the luxury of working remotely—they work because they need to put food on the table.

Bad enough that essential jobs put workers are at greater risk for infection, but some of those jobs, such as those at slaughterhouses and poultry processing plants, which President Trump ordered to be kept open, are dangerous. It's easy to demand that others accept low wages and put themselves at risk. The irony is stunning—essential and sometime dangerous work is rewarded with low wages. How does that make sense?

Workers who were employed at non-essential businesses actually caught a break by losing their jobs. By virtue of receiving state unemployment funds and $600 a week in federal benefits, some have been able—at least for a limited period of time—to pay their bills. But when economies opened up, these workers faced criticism for choosing unemployment benefits over returning to work.

Employers and some politicians blame the CARES Act for this predicament. What matters to them is that many employers who pay low wages can't compete with the CARES Act. As Sen. Rick Scott (R-Fla.) put it, "These employers are going to need these workers to rebuild this economy, so we cannot pay people more money on unemployment than what they would get in their jobs."

An episode some weeks back on talk radio, The Dave Ramsey Show, showed that employers are flabbergasted that employees would choose not to return to work. It's as if employees are doing something wrong by making a rational economic decision.

Saru Jayarman, president of One Fair Wage, an advocacy group, puts it this way: "They don't want the benefits to be easy to access because they want people willing to take low-wage jobs. We always want to keep a pool of low-wage labor at the ready."

Criticizing the CARES Act is easy work, but the CARES Act isn't to blame. It just brought to the forefront an issue we've been wrestling with for years.

Think about it, we've been paying a large segment of America low wages for years. Now, for the first time we've provided these workers with unemployment benefits that allow some modest degree of comfort, and we're stunned when they don't want to go back to work. Who in his right mind would decide differently?

Instead of looking at the CARES Act as the problem, why not change our mindset that wages for a certain sector of the economy must be kept low?

Support for change and a higher minimum wage is increasing across the nation, but there's still not enough support in Washington to make things happen. Worse yet, the opposition fails to present an alternate solution. Poor people are just left to be poor.

Sure, coming up with a solution is no easy task, and maybe there will be problems with raising wages. I don't know how to fix the problem, but I'm not willing to accept that the system must continue because, well, this is how capitalism operates.

And I'm bothered that those who say no to increasing the minimum wage are all employed and earning a good wage.

To restore Kimberly Parkway, we need human services first

April 27, 2020, The Columbus Dispatch

Duane Casares wants to restore Kimberly Parkway, a neighborhood on the southeast side of Columbus that surrounds the old Eastland Mall. "Kimberly has a terrible infant mortality problem and a high eviction rate. Many of its residents live at the federal poverty level ($26,200 for a family of four), are there are no youth-oriented services—libraries, recreation centers, YMCAs or Boys & Girls Clubs—anywhere."

Casares and the non-profit agency he heads, Direction for Youth and Families, work to strengthen families and transform communities. Now that DYF has been gifted an abandoned recreation center on Kimberly Parkway, Casares is focused on restoring the neighborhood—a heavy lift.

The first issue is dealing with unemployment. "If you're were unemployed while the economy was doing well, you're probably unemployable for lack of self-regulation, addiction and years of trauma that resulted from a variety of causes," Casares explains. "These folks don't need job training. They need to learn how to function in society. The job training comes later."

Next is education. "We've all heard that if you can't read by third grade, you're likely destined for a life of crime and prison, but that just speaks to correlation, not causation. A youngster's inability to read springs from various sources of dysfunction and stress in his life. We have to deal with those issues first."

After education comes housing, which brings us back to the poverty issue. Columbus enjoys a staggering low unemployment rate of 3.8 percent, but the number of residents living at twice the poverty level has been at or above 400,000 since 2010. Stated another way, too many people are employed at jobs that pay too little, and there isn't enough housing, meaning housing costs have been increasing at a rate that many residents can't afford.

Michael Wilkos, senior vice president at United Way of Central Way, sees the housing problem getting worse. "As Columbus' population grows, so does the number of people living in poverty. If Franklin County continues to grow at the same rate, by 2030, there will be over 200,000 new residents, a third of them will be living at twice the poverty level. Where will these additional low-income residents live?"

Even putting aside the poverty issue, not enough housing is being built. According to the local housing experts, Columbus needs 14,000 new housing units each year to meet population growth, but only 8,000 are produced annually.

When you combine increasing population, stagnant wages for workers at the bottom of the economic ladder and insufficient housing stock, neighborhoods change. A look at the past provides perspective.

Local economic think tank Regionomics calculated that in 1980, 40 percent of German Village residents and 34 percent of Victorian Village residents lived at the poverty level. By 2015, those percentages dropped to seven and 16, respectively.

The low-income earners didn't suddenly land higher paying jobs. They moved out because of escalating housing prices. Both neighborhoods are where they are today because of gentrification—a sudden influx of people with substantially higher incomes who bought modest and neglected houses and turned them into houses that command high prices.

The median price for a single-family residence in Columbus is $209,900, according to Columbus Realtors. The houses in German Village and Victorian Village have median values, according to Zillow, of $432,000 and $382,000, respectively.

Gentrification isn't an issue for Kimberly, but stagnant wages and increasing rents are. The median household income has barely moved since 2000. With an inflation rate of 46 percent since 2000, Kimberly residents have less buying power they did years ago, while the median rent in the area has increased from $560 to $732.

Local government is investing in affordable housing. Last year's increase in conveyance fees on real estate transactions is estimated to generate $6.5 million slated for affordable housing. The city passed a $50 million bond and has partnered with local corporations, philanthropic partners and government to raise a $100 million loan fund, all to support affordable housing.

The question is, will the bonds be enough? The second question is, how much more difficult will the coronavirus make it to restore Kimberly?

Guns

NRA needs to try a little flexibility
January 22, 2013, The Columbus Dispatch

What do the Great Oz and the National Rifle Association have in common? Both make a lot of noise and try to intimidate anybody who questions them, but unlike the Great Oz, the NRA has real power.

State Rep. Terry Johnson, R-McDermott, articulated the NRA's position in June 2012: "Our Second Amendment rights have been infringed countless times in the past. If we let someone come and take one right away from us … we diminish what it means to be an American."

Actually, Johnson is wrong. Over the last 200 years gun control has diminished. While guns have always been part of American culture, so too has gun control, states Adam Winkler in his book, Gunfight, the Battle Over the Right to Bear Arms in America. In the early 1800s, concealed carry was banned in Kentucky, Louisiana, Indiana, Tennessee and Virginia as a means to limit the potential for violence. Carrying firearms was once "strictly prohibited" in Dodge City, Ks., and most frontier towns used gun control to minimize violence and promote economic activity. Whatever restrictions may exist today, guns are readily accessible.

Winkler traces the history of the NRA and the conflict between the "gun grabbers" and the "gun nuts." When founded in 1871, the NRA's primary activity was to promote better marksmanship. The NRA's original slogan was "Firearms safety education, marksmanship training and shooting for recreation." Prior to serving as the NRA's president in the 1930s, Karl Frederick helped draft the Revolver Act of 1923, which required permits for concealed carry and required dealers to maintain records for handgun sales. The NRA supported legislation in 1934 and 1938 that taxed certain firearms, required gun registration and created a licensing system for gun dealers.

Things changed in 1977. The NRA's motto became, "The right of the people to keep and bear arms shall not be infringed," and any attempt at gun control is now viewed as an assault on the Second Amendment and a first step toward total gun confiscation. The NRA fought the Brady Bill and its five-day waiting period in 1993 and opposed a ban on bullets, known as cop killers, that can pierce Kevlar vests.

After the 1999 Columbine killings, the NRA didn't see a problem with the student-killers having evaded background checks by purchasing their guns from private dealers; the problem was that school officials weren't armed. No surprise, the NRA's response to Newtown, Conn., massacre is more guns, not limiting access to assault rifles.

Like all rights, Second Amendment rights are limited, a point the NRA is loath to admit.

When striking down the Washington, D.C., handgun law in District of Columbia v. Heller in 2008, Justice Antonin Scalia, wrote, "Nothing in our opinion should be taken to cast doubt on longstanding prohibitions on the possession of firearms by felons and the mentally ill, or laws forbidding the carrying of firearms in sensitive places such as schools and government buildings, or laws imposing conditions and qualifications on the commercial sale of arms."

The NRA can afford to be dogmatic. According to OpenSecrets.org, between 1989 and 2012 the NRA made political contributions of nearly $28 million and spent almost $19 million in political ads in the 2012 federal elections. The NRA also draws on the vocal strength of its members. Question whether more guns are a good idea, and you are subject to ugly personal attacks. I know from personal experience.

After challenging in The Dispatch whether more guns actually result in less crime, I was criticized on the web for "anti-rights bigotry" and "adolescent gamesmanship" and for "puking up a hackneyed, bigoted rant." The crowning blow, I was called the "idiot of the day" by someone who believes that guns are a "basic human right."

Even gun advocates are criticized when they advocate reason. Alan Gura, who argued for the gun owners in Heller, received several "vicious, nasty responses" from gun advocates. Why? Because he conceded before the court that machine guns are not protected by the Second Amendment. In Gura's words, the hard liners "are crazy."

Few politicians have the mettle to suffer caustic attacks from the NRA. It's safer to acquiesce to the NRA's very narrow dogma—and the campaign contributions are nice.

The challenge with dealing with the NRA is that it sees unfettered gun ownership as a way of addressing violence in America and posits the Second Amendment as the means to get there. That approach is wrongheaded. The question should be, how do we ensure that criminals and the mentally impaired do not have access to guns, and how do we reduce violence, all in a way that is consistent with the Second Amendment? This kind of discussion, however, requires the NRA to moderate its dogma.

Do people have the right to own any semiautomatic rifle, magazine size? Maybe not
March 29, 2013, The Columbus Dispatch

Are gun advocates right when they say they have a constitutional right to carry assault weapons such as the AR-15 and large capacity clips? Recent court decisions suggest not.

Until the U.S. Supreme Court reviewed in 2008 a handgun ban in District of Columbia v. Heller, it was unclear whether the Second Amendment was a collective or personal right.

The court's holding that the amendment conveys a personal right to own handguns was significant, but so too was how Justice Antonin Scalia expressly limited the court's holding. The Second Amendment is "not a right to keep and carry any weapon whatsoever in any manner whatsoever and for whatever purpose" and the government may prohibit "dangerous and unusual weapons."

In pronouncing this limitation, the court reflected on its holding in United States v Miller in 1939, where it upheld a ban on short-barreled shotguns. The Heller court saw its earlier decision to mean that "the Second Amendment does not protect those weapons not typically possessed by law-abiding citizens for lawful purposes."

So, do private citizens have the right to own assault weapons similar to those carried by modern day militia? Isn't there a connection in this awkwardly worded amendment between the prefatory clause—"A well regulated Militia, being necessary to the security of a free State"—and the operative clause—"the right of the people to keep and bear Arms, shall not be infringed?" Perhaps not.

The Heller court held that the government might have the right to limit ownership of "M-16 rifles and the like" even though these weapons "are most useful in military service." The connection between these phrases has diminished over time, as "modern developments have limited the degree of fit between the prefatory clause and the protected right."

In 2010, the court reviewed a Chicago handgun law similar to the one reviewed in Heller. Striking down the ordinance as unconstitutional in City of Chicago v. McDonald, the court went one step further and declared that the Second Amendment applies to state and local governments.

Still, the court repeated its limitation from Heller: "Nothing in our opinion should be taken to cast doubt on longstanding prohibitions on the possession of firearms by felons and the mentally ill, or laws forbidding the carrying of firearms in sensitive places such as schools and government buildings, or laws imposing conditions and qualifications on the commercial sale of arms."

These cases tell us we have a constitutional right to have a handgun in our homes for the purpose of self-defense, and that the government has the right to regulate possession and ban certain types of weapons. Where do assault weapons fit in?

We know from several federal appellate courts that machine guns fall outside the Second Amendment. Since 2008, three different federal appellate courts, citing Heller, have upheld bans on machine guns, referring to them as either "not typically possessed by law-abiding citizens for lawful purposes" or as "dangerous and unusual weapons."

So, are assault weapons like the AR-15, which are not fully automatic like machine guns, protected by the Second Amendment because they might be used for self-defense, or are they "dangerous and unusual weapons" that are "not typically possessed by law-abiding citizens for lawful purposes?"

Not surprising, the "gun grabbers" and "gun nuts" (terms coined by UCLA law professor Adam Winkler) view the Supreme Court decisions differently. Speaking on PBS after the McDonald case was decided, Paul Helmke, president of the Brady Campaign to Prevent Gun Violence, interpreted the cases to mean that "the extremes are off the table … you can't have gun bans, but you can't have this anybody, any gun, anywhere vision that I think [the National Rifle Association] pushes sometimes." Wayne LaPierre, executive vice president for the NRA, saw the cases as creating the opportunity for "restrictions and roadblocks" that "prevent the average citizen from getting access to this freedom."

The assault weapon question was answered by one court in 2011 in a second suit filed by Dick Heller, the plaintiff from the landmark Supreme Court case. This time, Heller challenged an ordinance that banned AR-15s and magazine clips that hold more than 10 rounds.

In a case often referred to as Heller II, the Court of Appeals for the District of Columbia upheld the ban. Quoting from Heller I, the court referred to AR-15s as "dangerous and unusual" and based its decision on the important government interest in "protecting police officers and controlling crime." Now back at the trial court, Heller II could conceivably find its way to the Supreme Court in a few years.

The issue isn't nearly as clear as the NRA blusters it is, and it's just possible the NRA is wrong.

Doctors must be able to ask about guns
September 18, 2013, The Columbus Dispatch

On July 30, state Sen. Kris Jordan, R-Powell, introduced
Sen. Bill 165, which would prohibit physicians from
asking patients questions about whether there are guns in
their home. What do guns have to do with a person's
health, and why should physicians care whether their
patients have guns?

Pediatricians ask these questions because guns are a
leading killer of children. The Children's Defense Fund
reported that in 2008 and 2009, 5740 children and teens,
including 299 children under age 10, were killed by
guns, and 8162 children and teens, including 847
children under age 10, were injured by guns. In 2008 and
2009, gun homicide was the leading cause of death for
black teens, ages 15 to 19; for white teens, ages 15 to 19,
it was vehicular accidents followed by gun homicide in
2008 and gun suicide in 2009.

"For a child, curiosity can be lethal, and guns spark
curiosity," states Robert Murray, MD, a pediatrician and
professor at The Ohio State University. "Pediatricians
are trained to evaluate environmental risks for children
and seek ways to minimize them. We help parents
understand that some of the things they take for granted
are real sources of danger for their children. Guns are a
public health issue for children, no different than
chemicals or electrical outlets."

Angela Sauaia, MD, who completed a study of children treated for gun injuries at two trauma centers, stated, "We didn't expect to see this many childhood injuries due to everyday gun violence … far too many of these were self-inflicted."

Florida passed a law similar to SB 165, but it was declared unconstitutional by a federal district court. The case is on appeal. The statute prohibits pediatricians, under penalty of loss of license, from asking questions or making any written record about firearms in the house. The Miami Herald reported that the bill was written by the NRA. According to court records, the statute was a response to a mother complaining her doctor told her she would need to find another doctor after she refused to answer questions about guns in her home.

The Florida statute permits questions about guns only when a physician believes "in good faith," that the information is relevant to a patient's safety. There is no similar provision in SB 165. As Florida physician Bernd Wollschlaeger, MD, points out, "You can only determine the relevance of the question once you have the answer."

Wollschlaeger, along with practically every medical association in Florida challenged the statute, which was struck down for violating the First Amendment right to free speech. The court held, "This law chills practitioners' speech in a way that impairs the provision of medical care and may ultimately harm the patient."

So, why would politicians ever think it good policy to suppress meaningful information about gun violence? The answer comes from former U.S. Rep. Jay Dickey. R-Ark, and Arthur Kellermann, MD: "Most politicians fear talking about guns almost as much as they would being confronted by one." Formerly an ardent gun advocate, Dickey has admitted that he once "served as the NRA's point person in Congress." Kellerman, formerly with the Center for Disease Control, published a study in the New England Journal of Medicine about guns in the home increasing the risk of homicide by a family member or acquaintance.

Murray agrees with the federal court's decision and sees real harm from SB 165. "As pediatricians, we don't care about guns themselves, but we do care about the danger they present to children. Too many kids get killed by guns. All we want to do is minimize that risk."

Murray thinks that clinical research is needed so that pediatricians can better understand gun-related injuries and develop sensible measures to insulate children from the harm of mishandled firearms. President Barack Obama has proposed $10 million in his 2014 budget to study gun violence prevention and convened a panel group to develop areas for study. The panel consists of members of the Institute of Medicine, National Research Council, American Association for the Advancement of Science, the CDC and several universities.

The panel's goal is "to provide a tool for the country to address this very difficult issue more productively than it has been able to do in the past." Its report states that "basic information about gun possession, distribution, ownership, acquisition and storage is lacking." The absence of good data makes it "virtually impossible to answer fundamental questions" about gun violence or programs that may reduce that violence.

We study highway collisions, airplane crashes, smoking, and HIV/AIDS, all for the purpose of saving lives. Why shouldn't we study gun violence, and why do we want to get in the way of how physicians treat their patients?

Focus needs to be on reducing gun deaths
April 21, 2014, The Columbus Dispatch

Almost every day we read about gun deaths. What's behind this problem? The National Rifle Association tells us, "Guns don't kill people. People kill people." Let's go with that. The FBI reports that in 2012, people killed 144 babies, 422 kids age 12 and under, 1327 teenagers, 96 husbands, 498 wives, 140 mothers, 126 fathers, 168 boyfriends, 494 girlfriends, and thousands of others, for a grand total of 12,723 people—with guns.

The numbers will not go down dramatically until we change our focus. If we're serious about reducing gun deaths, we need to stop debating whether more guns in the hands of law abiding citizens result in less crime. It's the wrong issue, and the evidence is inconclusive.

Economist John Lott was perhaps the first to champion the idea that more guns means less crime; others are in his camp. In response, scholars Ian Ayres and John J. Donohue III and others have refuted Lott's conclusion. The National Research Council concluded in 2004 that there is "no credible evidence that the passage of right-to-carry laws decreases or increases violent crime." The council also found that statistics concerning defensive gun use were unreliable because of "disagreement over the definition of defensive gun use and uncertainty over the accuracy of survey responses to sensitive questions and the methods of data collection."

Lott's credibility is also subject to question. He created a pseudonym, "Mary Rosh," a supposed former student, to defend his theories online. Posing as Rosh, Lott stated about himself online, "he was the best professor I ever had." Lott sued the publisher and one of the authors of Freakonomics in federal court for defamation concerning his research, but not about the Mary Rosh story. Upon reviewing the case, the appellate court found the Mary Rosh matter to be "an embarrassing charge, but one that was apparently true as Lott takes no issue with it in this case."

So, what's the best way to reduce how often "people kill people" with guns? Let's start analyzing how we can reduce gun deaths. David Hemenway, a professor at the Harvard School of Public Health, advocates treating gun violence as a public health issue. Forget about attributing blame for gun deaths. Hemenway suggests that we evaluate why certain segments of society are at risk and analyze how to prevent gun deaths for those groups.

Instead of focusing on the last person or opportunity that might have prevented a death, Hemenway says we should search several steps earlier in the chain of events for those opportunities that could have made a difference.

Part of the challenge is that we don't know enough about gun violence to immediately come up with answers. Complicating the problem is that gun violence is multi-faceted. CNN columnist LZ Granderson doesn't see a single cure for gun violence because each form of violence has its own unique characteristics. Think about it. People are shot in armed robberies, domestic violence, mass murders and gangland killings; children are killed by guns left unlocked, and guns are used to commit suicide.

What might work for one type of gun violence might not work for another. Banning assault weapons might help reduce mass murders, but assault weapons aren't the reason so many kids are killed when guns are left unattended. Requiring that weapons be locked at home might reduce the numbers of kids who are accidentally shot, but it won't change the number of deaths perpetrated by gang bangers. Background checks will help keep guns out of the hand of felons but won't do anything about stolen guns.

Columnist David Brooks believes we should start with a series of policies to reinforce gun-trafficking laws and reassert police control over zones of concentrated violence. The Department of Justice reports that over 230,000 guns are stolen each year. Based on polling data, Mayors Against Illegal Guns puts the number at 600,000. Exempt from federal licensing requirements, private sales do not require background checks, meaning countless guns are sold with no records.

A 2013 CNN documentary illustrated how easy a journalist could purchase three semi-automatic handguns and a semi-automatic rifle—no ID or paperwork required, no background check, and no possibility of tracing the weapons. The Bureau of Alcohol, Tobacco and Firearms reported in 2000 that during a 30 month period, it investigated traffickers who had diverted 84,128 firearms from legal to illegal commerce. Note how the ATF report begins: Virtually every gun used in a crime in the United States starts off as a legal firearm.

Arguing about whether guns are good or bad locks us in an emotional argument that goes nowhere. Let's start talking about reducing gun deaths and directing our efforts at research, analysis and changing norms.

Guns and kids

Winter 2014, Columbus Bar Association Lawyers Quarterly Magazine

What business does a doctor have asking his patients about guns? On July 30, state Sen. Kris Jordan, R-Powell, asked this question by introducing Sen. Bill 165, which would prohibit physicians from asking patients if there are guns in their home.

Not long ago, Florida passed a law similar to SB 165, which was declared unconstitutional last year in federal court. The case is on appeal. The Wisconsin State Journal reported on June 13, 2013, that a similar bill will be introduced in the Wisconsin legislature.

According to the American Academy of Pediatrics, the legislatures in Oklahoma, Tennessee, West Virginia and Virginia previously introduced bills that would restrict physicians from inquiring about firearms. Each bill failed to pass.

Wisconsin Rep. Michael Schraa stated, "Owning a firearm, or not owning a firearm, is a personal decision that has nothing to do with your physical health. Patients should not feel intimidated or harassed by their physicians over the exercise of a constitutional right."

Is Schraa right? Pediatricians don't think so. "For a child, curiosity can be lethal, and guns spark curiosity," stated Robert Murray, MD, a pediatrician and professor at The Ohio State University. "Pediatricians are trained to evaluate environmental risks for children and seek ways to minimize them. We help parents understand that some of the things they take for granted are real sources of danger for their children. Guns are a public health issue for children, no different than chemicals or electrical outlets."

Guns are a leading killer of children. The Children's Defense Fund reported that in 2008 and 2009, 5740 children and teens, including 299 children under age 10, were killed by guns, and 8162 children and teens, including 847 children under age 10, were injured by guns. In 2008 and 2009, gun homicide was the leading cause of death for black teens, ages 15 to 19; for white teens, ages 15 to 19, it was vehicular accidents followed by gun homicide in 2008 and gun suicide in 2009.

According to Jonathan Groner, MD, a pediatric surgeon and director of Nationwide Children's Hospital trauma program, from 2008 through 2012, Children's Hospital admitted 104 children for gunshot wounds, 29 of whom required care in the pediatric intensive care unit. Five of the injuries resulted in death. Seven injuries were self-inflicted, seven victims knew the shooter, and 10 other victims were related to the shooter. Twenty-eight children were shot in their homes, and 11 were shot at another home.

A New York Times article published on Sept. 28, 2013, revealed that roughly half of the accidental children shootings that were reviewed took place in the child's home, and a third occurred at a friend or relative's home.

Groner's personal experience is consistent with the Times article: "I have been reviewing the records of injured children for over 20 years, and it is extremely rare for a child to sustain a firearm injury from a criminal. In the vast majority of cases the children are shot by someone they know."

The Times article featured several examples of youngsters nationwide who were accidentally shot. A three-year old found a .45-caliber pistol that was hidden under a couch and shot himself in the eye. A 12-year old boy, mistakenly believing he had emptied all bullets from a pistol his father allowed him to use, shot his sister in the mouth. A nine-month old was killed when his two-year old brother grabbed a gun from a dresser drawer and squeezed the trigger.

The Times endeavored to identify every accidental gun death for children 14 and under in Georgia, Minnesota, North Carolina and Ohio dating to 1999 and in California to 2007. Cataloging 259 gun incidents, the Times "identified roughly twice as many accidental killings as were tallied in the corresponding federal data." The difference is attributed to inconsistencies in determining the cause of death. Circumstances characterized as accidental in one death may be characterized as homicide in another. The problem is that homicide is defined as the killing of another person, whether intentional or unintentional.

How deaths are characterized was the subject of a study conducted by the Harvard Injury Control Research

Center (Injury Prevention 2002; 8:252-256.). The study concluded that statistics "almost certainly underestimate the number of accidental firearm fatalities that occur each year, at least with respect to other inflicted shootings."

Lower estimates for accidental shootings provide the NRA with grounds for opposing safe storage laws and instead promoting "gun education." The NRA maintains that the number of accidental deaths for children has "decreased 89% since 1975. Today, the odds are more than a million to one, against a child in the U.S. dying in a firearm accident."

Groner disagrees. "The NRA numbers don't include death classified as homicides and suicides. The NRA does not count these children, but they matter. There is ample data to suggest that the availability of a firearm in the home greatly increases the risk of homicide and suicide among children. Public health experts believe that if guns were not so accessible, these deaths would not occur."

Gaining accurate information about accidental deaths is impeded by the NRA's long- running battle against about gun violence research, which began in 1993. That year, the New England Journal of Medicine published a study about guns in the home increasing the risk of being shot by a family member or acquaintance. The lead researcher was Arthur Kellermann, MD, who was with the Center for Disease Control.

Seeing the study as an attack on gun rights, the NRA
pushed to eliminate federal funding for gun studies.
Former Rep. Jay Dickey, R-Ark, spearheaded legislation
in 1996, known as the "Dickey Amendment," that
prohibits the CDC from using its funding "to advocate or
promote gun control." While not explicitly prohibiting
research on gun violence, the legislation effectively
stopped it. "Precisely what was or was not permitted
under the clause was unclear," Kellermann said, "but no
federal employee was willing to risk his or her career or
the agency's funding to find out."

After the National Institute of Health published a 2009
study investigating the link behind gun possession and
gun assault, Congress extended the equivalent of the
Dickey amendment to the NIH. The NRA sees gun
research as "junk science designed to paint legal gun
ownership as a public health hazard."

Dickey, who admitted he once "served as the NRA's
point person in Congress," later had an epiphany. In July
2012, he and Kellermann co-authored an op-ed piece in
The Washington Post, that questioned "why we know
more and spend so much more on preventing traffic
fatalities than on preventing gun violence, even though
firearm deaths (31,347 in 2009, the most recent year for
which statistics are available) approximate the number of
motor vehicle deaths (32,885 in 2010)."

Dickey and Kellermann maintain that, without research,
scientists cannot answer basic questions about how best
to prevent gun deaths. "The same evidence-based

approach that is savings millions of lives from motor vehicle crashes as well as from smoking, cancer and HIV/AIDS, can help reduce the toll of deaths and injuries from gun violence."

So, why would politicians ever think it good policy to suppress meaningful information about gun violence? According to Dickey and Kellermann, "Most politicians fear talking about guns almost as much as they would being confronted by one."

Murray sees real harm from SB 165. "As pediatricians, we don't care about guns themselves, but we do care about the danger they present to children. Too many kids get killed by guns. All we want to do is minimize that risk."

Groner agrees. "Most pediatricians talk to parents and their children about car seats and other dangers that exist in everyday life. It is unreasonable to forbid doctors from discussing firearms and firearm safety, when firearms kill so many children."

Gun rights aren't at risk in gun-safety laws that protect children's lives
March 24, 2017, The Cleveland Plain Dealer (on-line)

Florida pediatricians had a good day in court last month when the U.S. Court of Appeals for the 11th Circuit struck down on First Amendment grounds a statute that prohibited them from addressing gun safety with parents. The battle over a pediatrician's right to freely practice medicine and protect the safety of children was one that never should have occurred, but Florida legislators thought it necessary to protect gun rights when, in fact, gun rights were never threatened.

The legal conflict began in 2011, when several pediatricians and medical associations challenged the statute in federal court. In 2012, the court held the law was unconstitutional because it infringed on free speech. After a three-judge panel of the 11th Circuit reversed the trial court's decision in 2014, the pediatricians asked the court's entire panel of 11 judges to hear the case. The full panel affirmed the trial court's decision, meaning pediatricians may resume talking about gun safety.

To pediatricians, asking about guns is no different than asking about chemicals, electrical outlets or swimming pools. They're all a source of danger for kids.

Pediatricians inquire about guns because some parents don't understand the risk and lack knowledge about safe storage. There's evidence to support the pediatricians' concerns. The Children's Defense Fund reported that

883 children and teens nationwide died in 2010 from gun suicide and accidental shootings; 143 were 14 and under. From 2000 through 2010, 384 Florida children died from gun suicide and 54 from accidental shootings.

What was striking about the law is that it was based on six anecdotal stories presented by legislators. Legislators testified about their constituents being subjected to unwelcome questions or comments about gun ownership. One legislator testified that a mother was separated from her children while medical personnel interrogated them about guns. Significantly, the court record reflected, "There was no other evidence, empirical or otherwise, presented to or cited by the Florida legislature" about harm suffered by gun owners.

Florida isn't alone in trying to suppress physicians. In 2013 and 2015, Sen. Kris Jordan, R-Ostrander, introduced similar bills in Ohio that, fortunately, went nowhere. In January, state Sen. Bob Hall, R-Edgewood, introduced comparable legislation in Texas.

These efforts are misguided. Not everything that deals with guns touches on the Second Amendment.

The National Rifle Association disagrees. It views the pediatricians' practice as an attack on guns and an invasion of privacy. Chris Cox, executive director for the NRA's Institute for Legislative Action, lauded the first decision from the 11th Circuit. "Every gun owner in Florida and across the country is grateful for this common sense ruling. It is not a physician's business whether his or her patient chooses to exercise their fundamental, individual right to own a firearm."

Cox is right—to an extent. It's not a physician's business whether a parent owns a gun, but it is a physician's concern that parents be knowledgeable about the dangers some take for granted. Children who shoot themselves and others do so only because an adult left a loaded gun where it could be easily found.

The reality is, gun rights were never at risk in Florida. Patients were always free to refuse to answer questions about guns. Moreover, as the full panel of the 11th Circuit noted, the Second Amendment "does not preclude questions about, commentary on, or criticism for the exercise of that right."

Ironically, Florida passed a statute in 1989 that made it a misdemeanor to fail to secure guns that are obtained by minors without supervision. In passing the statute, the legislature recognized that "a tragically large number of Florida children have been accidentally killed or seriously injured by negligently stored firearms" and "that placing firearms within the reach or easy access of children is irresponsible." If anything, the pediatricians were endeavoring to meet the legislature's public safety concerns articulated years prior.

The Florida statute illustrates how a legislature and the NRA can lose sight of the fact that hundreds of kids who are killed annually when guns are left out in the open. Gun rights aren't at risk. The lives of children are, and those lives are all the pediatricians care about.

Legislating gun bills: lots of storytelling, little data

Fall 2017, Columbus Bar Association Lawyers Quarterly
[Co-authored with Jeffrey Eyerman]

The Ohio General Assembly seems to be enamored with guns. And laws designed to get them into more people's hands. At least six pending bills seek to expand the rights of gun owners in general, and concealed carry holders in particular. The proposals range from the practical (H.B. 152 proposes a "firearm restriction" be added to the hunting licenses of convicted felons) to the questionable (H.B. 201 would allow anyone to carry a concealed weapon without a permit and eliminate the obligation to tell the police you're carrying).

The General Assembly seems to be proceeding on the premise that more guns in hands of citizens is a good thing, but the data — notably lacking in the hearings for these bills — suggests otherwise. Unlike courts which require hard evidence, lawmakers propose legislation based on what makes a good story. Here are a few examples:

H.B. 233 would allow all concealed carry holders or, if permitting requirements disappear, anyone to carry their guns into schools, courthouses and daycares, so long as they leave when requested. In introducing the bill, Rep. John Becker (R-Clermont), has referred to concealed carry holders as the "cream of the crop of the citizenry," noting that concealed carry holders "are required to pass a background check, be fingerprinted, photographed and trained in gun safety and marksmanship."[1] It's unclear how these requirements elevate one's status. After all, folks who get arrested are fingerprinted, background checked and photographed, and some probably underwent gun training.

Mr. Becker seems to have resolved this dissonance with what he amusingly calls the "jerk clause." That is, "if [when asked to leave], you choose to be a jerk about it and refuse to leave, you are then subject to the charge of disorderly conduct." Why give anyone the opportunity to be a jerk about it in the first place? The reasoning isn't clear, nor is the benefit that society gains from more concealed guns in more public places.

Some lawmakers seemingly want to make it easier for people to use their guns. Rep. Sarah M. LaTourette (R-Chesterland), has co-sponsored H.B. 228, which shifts the burden of proof in criminal prosecutions involving claims of self-defense. A type of "stand-your-ground" law, the proposed bill would require prosecutors, in cases where an accused shooter claims self-defense, to prove beyond a reasonable doubt that the shooter was *not* acting in self-defense.

To LaTourette's mind, the law would ensure that "law-abiding citizens in our state don't have to try to decide if they will be able to defend themselves in court before they decide to defend their family in a life and death

---

[1] Testimony offered by Rep. John Becker on June 6, 2017.

situation."[2] LaTourette doesn't tell us how often this situation arises, though it certainly occurs — recall that a judge in Jefferson County was recently attacked and defended himself by returning fire. As we'll discuss later on, those instances when citizens actually use a gun in self-defense may be rarer than you think.

Rep. Nino Vitale (R-Urbana) is sponsoring H.B. 310, a bill that would let elected officials carry guns into their places of business. It's a sensible enough policy on its face, but Vitale's rhetoric is a bit unsettling. As he sees it, "if someone knows someone can defend themselves, they might keep their rhetoric at an acceptable level."[3] Does this mean, people who protest against public officials might need to stay quiet or risk being shot by their representatives?

What does the data say about right to carry (RTC) laws and their effect on crime? Little, until recently. A 2004 report from the National Academies National Research Council concluded "it is not possible to reach any scientifically supported conclusion. … The evidence to date does not adequately indicate either the sign or the magnitude of a causal link between the passage of right-to-carry laws and crime rates. Furthermore, this uncertainty is not likely to be resolved with the existing data and methods."[4]

---

[2] Testimony offered by Rep. Sarah M. LaTourette on June 20, 2017.
[3] The Columbus Dispatch, July 28, 2017
[4] "Firearms and violence, a critical review," Committee to Improve Research Information and Data on Firearms,

Since then, Stanford Law Professor John Donohue has concluded, using a new statistical technique, that on average, RTC states have violent crime rates that were seven percent *higher* five years after RTC law passage than non-RTC states during the same five years. After 10 years, the gap increased to almost 15 percent. "There is not even the slightest hint in the data that RTC laws reduce overall violent crime," Donohue stated.[5]

Donohue makes an interesting analogy concerning widespread gun ownership: "If we gave 300 million people a brain scan, we would save a certain number of lives, but you wouldn't want to advocate that treatment without considering how many lives would be lost by exposing so many to radiation damage. One needs to consider both the costs and benefits of any treatment or policy."

What costs come with gun proliferation? The data suggests that more guns in a home increase the likelihood of those guns being used to murder family members. In a study published in 1993, researchers studied 1,860 murders in three Tennessee, Washington and Ohio counties.[6] Of those murders, 420 occurred in

---

Charles F. Wellford, John V. Pepper, and Carol V. Petrie, editors, National Research Council of the National Academies, executive summary at p. 7.
[5] http://news.stanford.edu/2017/06/21/violent-crime-increases-right-carry-states/
[6] "Gun Ownership as a Risk Factor for Homicide in the Home," New England Journal Medicine, October 7, 1993;

the home of the victim, with 76.7 percent of the victims killed by a relative or someone known to them. Homicide by stranger accounted for just 3.6 percent of the home murders.

FBI statistics also evidence that most victims are murdered by someone they know. Of the 7,023 homicides (involving both guns and other weapons) in 2015 where the assailant was identified, the victims were murdered by strangers in only 1,375 cases. The other 5,648 murders were committed by relatives or acquaintances.[7]

Arthur L. Kellermann, Frederick P. Rivara, Norman B. Rushforth, Joyce G. Banton, Donald T. Reay, Jerry T. Francisco, Ana B. Locci, Janice Prodzinski, Bela B. Hackman, and Grant Somes.

King County, Tenn., was largely white and enjoyed a relatively high standard of living. Shelby County, Wash, and Cuyahoga County, Ohio, were 44 and 25 percent black, respectively. Fifteen percent of Shelby County households lived below the poverty level. Eleven percent of Cuyahoga County's households lived below the poverty level. The homicides in King and Shelby counties occurred over a five-year period. The homicides in Cuyahoga County occurred during a two and a half year period.

[7] https://ucr.fbi.gov/crime-in-the-u.s/2015/crime-in-the-u.s.-2015/tables/expanded_homicide_data_table_10_murder_circumstan ces_by_relationship_2015.xls

https://ucr.fbi.gov/crime-in-the-u.s/2015/crime-in-the-u.s.-2015/tables/expanded_homicide_data_table_8_murder_victims_by_ weapon_2011-2015.xls

Increased gun availability also increases the risk of gun suicide. The Centers for Disease Control reported 21,334 gun suicides in 2014.[8] Researchers have found that "victims of suicide living in homes with guns were more than 30 times more likely to have died from a firearm-related suicide than from one committed with a different method." Why? Because guns require little preparation — an important attribute, "particularly when the suicide is impulsive."[9]

And how often are guns used in self-defense? While advocates have claimed that 2.5 million Americans use guns in self-defense each year, Harvard's David Hemenway has concluded this number is way off and based on faulty data. Survey respondents claim to have shot more than 200,000 criminals, but only about 100,000 people are treated in emergency rooms for all gunshot wounds annually — including criminals, who "almost all go to hospital emergency rooms for treatment of their wounds."[10]

If law-abiding gun owners fatally shot 200,000 criminals annually, they would be doing away with 3,846 bad hombres per week. Yet, FBI statistics for 1993 show

---

[8] https://www.cdc.gov/nchs/fastats/suicide.htm
[9] "Guns in the Home and Risk of a Violent Death in the Home," Linda L. Dahlberg, Robin M. Ikeda, Marcie-jo Kresnow, American Journal of Epidemiology, Volume 160, Issue 10, Nov. 15, 2004, pp. 929–936.
[10] "Private Guns, Public Health," David Hemenway, Univ. of Michigan Press, 2006, at p. 68.

only 350 justifiable homicides by citizens — fewer than seven per week.

None of this is to say every gun bill should always be dead on arrival. The quite-reasonable H.B. 253, for example, would allow off-duty police officers to carry their weapons into otherwise "gun-free" zones. One could also see the sense in allowing elected officials a modicum of additional security by allowing them to take concealed weapons into government facilities.

But legislators, eager to ease concealed carry restrictions and make it harder for police and prosecutors to do their jobs, could learn something from the courts: rely on facts instead of storytelling when passing bills. We'd probably all be safer in the long run if they did.

More guns alone not the answer
October 2, 2017, the Columbus Dispatch

Are we safer by making it easier for citizens to carry guns? The Ohio General Assembly thinks so. At least six bills seek to expand the rights of gun owners. There's ample data to suggest that more guns don't promote safety and that with more guns the number of unintended deaths increases.

Legislators don't seem to care about data. Then maybe they should take a minute and listen to what fighter pilots have to say about self-defense in the air.

Fighter pilots live by the paradigm, "Keep your head on a swivel." It's the enemy aircraft you don't see that will shoot you down. Some 80 to 90 percent of downed pilots never see their attacker—until it's too late. Tied to this paradigm is, "The first guy to get a missile in the air wins." Start a dogfight in a defensive posture, and you'll likely die.

How do these paradigms relate to guns and self-defense? All the guns in the world won't save you if you're not alert to your surroundings. If guns alone were the answer, we wouldn't have armed police officers being ambushed and killed.

On occasion we hear about an armed citizen stopping a shooter, but those situations likely involve a shooter who was caught off guard. An armed judge in Steubenville,

Ohio, with help from a probation officer, killed his attacker, but that's the exception.

A third fighter pilot paradigm is, "fight like you train." When the shooting starts, it's too late to think about how to maneuver your jet. If you're unable to react instinctively, you're going to die. Fighter pilots regularly practice aerial combat maneuvering, memorize the capabilities of their weapons, and study the strengths and weaknesses of enemy aircraft.

If you don't regularly engage in repetitive training under a variety of high stress scenarios and think you can take out a shooter and not kill or wound bystanders, your arrogance will be your undoing.

Time Magazine carried a sobering article on Jan. 16, 2013, about how the brain reacts and bullets get sprayed in gunfights. New York city cops involved in gun fights typically hit their targets only 18% of the time. When they fired at a shooter outside the Empire State Building in the summer of 2012, they put 10 bullets in him but also hit nine bystanders.

The story of a gun fight in an apartment illustrates how disorienting things become when the shooting starts. While running for cover and dragging his wounded partner, veteran Chicago cop Jim Glennon didn't realize he had dropped his gun. After taking cover behind a corner, Glennon pointed at the shooter with what he thought was his gun, but he was just holding his hand

out in front of him, pointing it in the shape of gun like a
kid at play.

Responding to the question whether teachers should be
armed, Glennon expressed his concern. "Cops aren't
trained well enough, so what do you think they're going
to do with the teachers? It's not enough to carry a gun."
Ryan Millerbern, a former policer officer in Colorado,
talks about how he has struggled under gunfire to
perform basic functions. He thinks it's "very unrealistic"
to assume armed teachers would perform competently in
a gunfight.

The gun lobby has created the fiction that "only a good
guy with a gun can stop a bad gun with a gun." The
reality is, a gun will protect you only if you don't let the
bad guy get the drop on you. But it's impossible to be
vigilant all the time. Full-time vigilance would freeze
your ability to do anything else.

What's the answer? The nation has to become proactive.

The gun lobby says that by carrying a gun, you're being
proactive. No, being proactive means taking steps to
prevent a problem from occurring. Let's be proactive
and get the guns out of the hands of bad guys.

Mandating background checks for all gun sales would be
a good start. Recognizing that gun violence is a public
health issue—some 30,000 people die annually from gun
homicides and suicides—and funding research of the
factors that contribute to gun violence would be a good

second step. Next, the Bureau of Alcohol, Tobacco and Firearms should have an updated system to track the source of guns used in crimes; the present system is inadequate.

But the gun lobby doesn't like any of these ideas. Its existence and financial well-being depend on inciting fear and spreading the fiction that more guns alone are the answer.

U.S. should study gun violence as a public health hazard

November 13, 2017, The Columbus Dispatch

We've been taking two ineffective approaches to gun violence. The first is to debate whether we need more or fewer guns. Fearing criticism for not supporting the Second Amendment, legislators are easily persuaded we need more guns.

The second approach occurs after a mass shooting. A new gun law is proposed. We argue its merits, and then Second Amendment concerns swallow the process, and nothing changes.

We've got things backwards. We need to research and understand gun violence. Only then can we craft realistic solutions that comply with the Second Amendment.

Note to gun enthusiasts: the Second Amendment doesn't provide unlimited gun rights. At least four federal appellate courts have held that bans on "assault" weapons are constitutional.

Let's start by evaluating what we want. According to the Centers for Disease Control, the U.S. had 12,979 gun homicides, 84,997 gun injuries and 22,979 gun suicides in 2015. Is this acceptable?

The CDC tells us 629 children, age 11 and younger, were killed or injured by guns in 2015, as were 6985 teens, ages 12-17. Is this what we want?

Everytown for Gun Safety calculates that from 2009 to 2016 we had 156 mass shootings—four or more people killed, excluding the shooter—where 848 people were killed and another 339 were injured. Fifty-four percent of mass shootings are related to domestic violence, and in a third of the shootings, the shooter was prohibited from possessing firearms. Is that okay?

Until we agree on what type of society we want, we can't make policy decisions. Some will argue violence is part of the human condition, a reality we have to accept. Nonsense!

We're not so fatalistic about other types of crimes. We legislate to effect control over what threatens us. We didn't accept polio or automobile deaths as beyond our control. If we were to lose 30,000 people annually to aviation crashes, we wouldn't wring our hands and lament over the power of gravity.

Because of the gun lobby, Congress put the cuffs on the CDC in researching gun violence. Let's study gun violence like we study every other public health hazard, and let's talk about the costs that come with more guns.

More guns means more gun violence. In the study he conducted, Michael Siegel, M.D. of the Boston University School of Health, found a "robust correlation" between estimated levels of gun ownership and actual gun homicides. For each percentage point increase in gun ownership, the gun homicide rate increases by 0.9 percent.

More guns means more women die from guns. Siegel also found that for every 10 percent increase in gun ownership, the gun homicide rate for women increases at the same rate.

More guns mean more gun suicides. A study published in the American Journal of Epidemiology found that suicide victims living in homes with guns were more than 30 times more likely to have died from a gun than other means.

More guns—maybe more opportunities for kids to shoot themselves and others?

More guns likely means more guns will be stolen. According to the Harvard School of Public Health, some 200,000 to 500,000 guns are stolen annually. Where do you think those guns end up? The Bureau of Alcohol, Tobacco and Firearms is hamstrung trying trace guns used in crimes. We don't have a national database for most guns, and the ATF's resources for tracing guns is outdated.

Guns serve many useful purposes, but their use comes at great cost, a fact our politicians fail to grasp. Enough with thoughts and prayers. It's time to recognize gun violence for what it is—a public health hazard.

Unsecured firearms lead to accidental deaths in children
Winter 2017, Ohio Pediatrics

Unsecured guns and children make for a bad mix, and there is a great deal more we can do to keep children safe from accidental gun injuries. Here is what has been happening in Ohio:

> - June 25, 2016, Cleveland: a 10-year-old boy accidentally shot an 8-year-old boy.
> - July 16, 2016, Cincinnati: a 7-year-old boy was accidentally shot to death.
> - August 28, 2016, Dayton: a 7-year-old boy was shot in the leg after he and his friends found a gun inside a shed.
> - Oct. 23, 2016, Columbus: a 10-year-old boy was accidentally shot when he and his friends found a gun.

Between Jan. 1, 2014, and June 30, 2016, there were 74 accidental shootings in Ohio involving children; 19 children died. Nationwide during this period, over 320 minors age 17 and under and more than 30 adults were killed in accidental shootings involving minors. Nearly 700 children and adults were injured, and nearly 90 3-year-olds were either killed or injured. These numbers come from an analysis by the Associated Press and USA Today of data collected by Gun Violence Archive, a non-partisan research group.

What's the answer? A combination of education and safe storage.

Children need to be taught that guns are items to be avoided when adults are not around. We teach kids to look both ways before crossing the street, not to stick their fingers into electrical outlets, etc. Gun safety should be part of that discussion.

But education isn't enough, because kids are curious, and guns are a source of great curiosity, a point illustrated by an experiment ABC News conducted in January 2014 at a preschool and child care center (with parental consent) in St. Petersburg, Fla. (http://abcnews.go.com/WNT/video/ hidden-camera-experiment-children-drawn-guns-found- classroom-22258370)

Youngsters, whose parents own guns, were shown the NRA's Eddie Eagle video and instructed by a police officer what to do if they found a gun. The message was reinforced by a teacher. A few days later, the officer hid an unloaded gun in the classroom. Eddie Eagle is an animated figure who teaches kids, when they find a gun, to "Stop! Don't Touch. Leave the area. Tell an adult."

What did the kids do when they found the gun? They recited the "don't touch" mantra but proceeded to touch the gun. Two boys looked straight down the barrel—and then called for an adult.

Surprising? It shouldn't be. Guns are too much of a temptation. Plus, parents aren't good at hiding things, and kids are stronger than we think. Nationwide Children's Hospital tells us that, notwithstanding what parents may think, eight of 10 first graders know where their parents store their guns, and a three-year-old can pull the trigger on most American guns.

According to ABC News, there is a gun in one out of every three homes. So, even if you're a parent who vigilantly safeguards his firearms, your child can still be at risk when visiting a friend.

What to do? For these reasons, education has to be supplemented with safe storage. At a minimum, lock your guns and keep them out of reach of kids. Understand how tempting it is for kids to play with guns. Advocate for safe storage of firearms combined with education to protect children.

In Ohio, we are beginning to take steps toward safer gun storage and education for families. The Kiwanis Club of Columbus, Ohio, recently donated $10,000 to the Ohio AAP for the purchase of gun boxes. When pediatricians talk with parents about protecting their children from the lethal hazards that exist in every house—cleaning chemicals, electrical outlets, etc.— parents will be asked if they have a means to safely store their guns. A gun box will be given to those parents who do not.

I've examined one of those gun boxes. It's locked by a key and takes almost no time to unlock. I suppose some will say that even the second or two it takes to unlock a gun box is too much time when your life is at stake. Maybe. But if a bad guy has that big of a drop on you, that second or two probably won't mean much of a difference anyway.

Any parent who has lost a child to an accidental shooting would likely give up that second or two to have his child back.

This pilot program is supported by the Buckeye Firearms Association, Black Wing Shooting Center, and injury prevention advocates from around the state. We are bringing together all sides of the issue to find common-sense solutions for what we all agree on–kids should be safe around guns.

The support of the Kiwanis Club of Columbus to make this program happen is a reminder of what can be achieved when the community becomes involved in keeping kids healthy. There is great evidence that a partnership between the AAP and Kiwanis can save thousands of children's lives. In the 1950s, these two groups led the effort to spread the polio vaccine, eradicating the disease in the USA by 1980.

I hope the partnership of the Ohio AAP and Kiwanis Club of Columbus is the beginning of another historical movement to save children's lives.

**Citizens and lawmakers all can work
to combat gun violence**
August 24, 2019, The Columbus Dispatch

If you're not outraged by the nation's gun violence, you
should be. If you're outraged but doing nothing,
recognize that your inaction contributes to the problem.
If you're a state or U.S. lawmaker who follows the gun
lobby script, it's time to acknowledge that gun violence
is a public health issue.

Here are suggestions for both concerned citizens and
lawmakers. First, the suggestions for citizens.

1. Understand what works. The gun lobby wields
power because it knows that money talks and its
members are vocal and loud. Politicians listen when
campaigns contributions are on the line, and theyfear
the wrath of angry gun zealots.

2. Get involved. Join a gun policy group—Moms
Demand Action for Gun Sense in America, Sand Hook
Promise, Everytown for Gun Safety or the Ohio
Coalition Against Gun Violence—and learn about
pending gun issues. Donate and help fund the cause.

3. Get vocal. Contact your legislators about pending
gun legislation. Send emails or call. Make it known
what bills you support and which you consider to be
dangerous.

4. Use social media. Facebook isn't just for anniversaries and cute puppies. Educate your friends about pending gun bills and ask them to get involved.

5. vote out the legislators who have been seduced by the siren song of the gun lobby. They're easy to recognize. They're mostly Republicans.

Suggestions for lawmakers:

1. Acknowledge that the majority of Americans want a safer world. The people who fight all gun restrictions, no matter how reasonable, are a minority.

What matters is a legal analysis of the Second Amendment. While the meaning of those 27 words is not readily clear, they certainly don't mean that all Americans are entitled to possess all types of guns, all the time and everywhere, no matter the situation.

2. disregard the gun lobby's propaganda. The gun lobby wants you to believe that any restriction on gun ownership violates the Second Amendment. Not true. Courts have consistently held that reasonable restrictions are constitutional.

3. Mandate background checks for all weapon transfers and expand the three-day waiting period to conduct those checks.

4. Make decisions based on evidence. The gun lobby offers lots of anecdotes but little evidence about why more guns is a good idea. Forget the fiction that more guns promote safety and pay attention to research. States with universal background checks have lower pediatric firearm-related mortality rates. More firearms in homes means an increased risk of women being shot by their significant other. And as a recent study shows, as concealed carry permits increase, so does violent crime.

5. The U.S. suffers from at least seven types of gun violence: murders committed in the commission of a felony, domestic violence, gangland violence, mass murders, serial killings, accidental shootings of children, and suicide. Each has its own unique set of dynamics, and we know little about each. There's no one fix for this array of violence.

6. Adopt a strategy of being proactive. The gun lobby's approach to gun violence is reactive—more people should carry guns. That's akin to battling disease by simply doling out penicillin to the sick, instead of getting ahead of the problem and teaching good hygiene and health habits and inoculating people.

7. Follow the guns. We have virtually no system in place to trace guns used in crimes.

8. Recognize sophistry when you see it. The gun lobby's mantra for opposing gun legislation—"Guns

don't kill people; people kill people."—is silly. Of course, inanimate objects by themselves don't kill, but in the hands of the people, guns caused over 39,000 deaths in 2017. That's why we need reasonable restrictions on what guns people can access.

How We Treat Each Other

Former POW has learned not to hate
May 26, 2014, The Columbus Dispatch

Sometimes the lessons we learn aren't what we would
expect. You would expect to hear about faith or courage
from a former prisoner of war. You wouldn't expect a
POW to talk about the destructive nature of hate, but
that's the lesson from Tom Moe, a Capital University
graduate and Vietnam War POW, who served as
Director of the Ohio Department of Veterans Services
from 2010 to 2013.

Moe's lesson for us is one of three ironies within his
story, and, as we celebrate Memorial Day, it's
appropriate to learn from him.

Moe's F-4 Phantom went down in January of 1968 in the
Vietnam War. The first irony is that he wasn't downed
by the enemy. His wingman was carrying a bomb with a
faulty fuse, a relatively inexpensive item that detonated
prematurely; the bomb exploded while airborne,
destroying two multi-million dollar jets and forcing four
aircrew to eject.

Moe spent three days in the cold, wet jungle evading the
enemy. After being discovered hiding under a log, Moe
was forced to march 100 miles to a POW camp. The trek
was difficult but tolerable.

Once Moe arrived at the camp, his world was turned
upside down, starting with nine months of solitary
confinement and torture. POWs were regarded as war

criminals and subject to one rule: "Criminals will strictly follow all regulations or will be severely punished."

Not providing military information when interrogated was a violation of the rule and resulted in torture. That meant sitting on a stool for 24 hours a day for 10 days straight. Sometimes Moe would be tied to the stool, with his wrists strapped to his ankles. Sometime he was not tied, but forbidden to move. If he moved, other than to use a waste bucket in the corner, he would be beaten with fists and gun butts until the guards tired.

Other times, Moe was forced to stand immobile "around the clock," and then kneel for up to six hours at a time, a process that went on for days. This was supposed to motivate him to sign a war confession, but Moe refused, which led to 20 guards beating him. After that, he was waterboarded.

Here's the second irony. America was outraged when we later learned how men had been tortured in Vietnam, but we later waterboarded the prisoners at Guantanamo Bay. Former Vice President Dick Cheney characterized it as "enhanced interrogation," but that's a story for another day.

There were more beatings that caused internal bleeding and broken ribs. Moe was gaunt, his skin festered with rashes and fungus, and his eye sockets were "two puffy slits." Poking your finger into his flesh would leave a hole that would slowly fill with fluid. He was given little to eat and putrid water to drink and lived in a barren cell, sometimes shared with rats.

Finally, the beatings lessened, and Moe knew he was "over the hump," which brings us to the third irony in Moe's story, his thoughts about hate: "I had to cope with one of the most corrosive elements of the human spirit—hate. Hate is a terrible distraction, a horribly destructive human enterprise. Hate invades the consciousness when the mind's reasoning power fades. Hate is a way we assign blame for our plight when our faith weakens and our resolve becomes clouded. Pain intensifies hate, making us want to strike out at something." A fascinating concept from a man who we would think is justified in hating his captors.

Look around you and it should become clear that Moe's lesson is relevant to us. We're no longer just a society of differing views. We're a society that is divided into several camps of strident views where people refuse to find common ground and instead engage in endless exchanges of angry rhetoric.

Try this experiment: turn on the TV but turn off the volume. It doesn't matter what you're watching or that you can't hear the words. You'll see angry faces. Whatever the news story— taxes, abortion, immigration, guns—it's all the same. People will be talking—no, yelling—at each other. If that isn't hate you're watching, it's just a shade less.

This hate—or whatever you want to call it—clouds our thinking and weakens us. It prevents us from reaching consensus because it makes enemies out of those with whom we disagree, and once we have created enemies— well, you can't give in, because they're enemies. Of course, no one wants to call it hate. It's "fighting for principle," they'll say. No, Moe was fighting for principle. We're squandering precious time hating.

Community-based care is better for disabled Ohioans
November 6, 2014, The Toledo Blade

Concerned that nursing homes are becoming a dumping ground for the mentally disabled, Ohio has expanded a trial program that will transfer 2000 people with behavioral problems from nursing homes to managed community settings. Opposing this idea are—you guessed it—the nursing homes.

Disability Rights Ohio, the state's advocacy system for the disabled, believes that over 8000 people with behavioral problems are improperly placed in nursing homes. "The number has grown significantly in the last 10 to 15 years," says Michael Kirkman, DRO's executive director. "With proper support, many of these individuals could live in the community."

Several factors contribute to the problem, including changes in funding for mental health services and cuts in federal spending for subsidized housing. Placing people with disabilities in nursing homes is an easy solution for some caregivers, says Kirkman, and high vacancy rates in nursing homes results in these facilities advertising their ability to deal with "problem residents" in secure "behavioral units."

DRO maintains that residents in these units are isolated and have no contact with the outside and, because of anomalies in Medicaid, they do not receive services from community mental health services. Care is typically poor and often consists solely of medication. DRO believes that home and community-based services are more effective, more humane and less expensive.

Failure to ensure that the disabled are served in the most integrated setting appropriate to their needs is a violation of the Americans with Disabilities Act. In 1999, the U.S. Supreme Court held in *Olmstead v. L.C.* that states must provide community-based treatment for people with disabilities when the state's treatment professionals determine that placement is appropriate, the disabled do not object, and placement can be reasonably accommodated in light of state resources.

Based on the *Olmstead* case, the federal court here in Columbus was asked to rule on a class action, where the lead plaintiff, Nancy Martin, was a 52-year old woman who suffered from cerebral palsy, mental disabilities and depression. She had lived in institutional settings for more than 30 years after being involuntarily committed to a developmental center when her father died and her mother was unable to care for her. Martin's efforts in communicating to case workers that she wanted to live in a community setting were futile. Her name was placed on a waiting list, where it remained for years.

Martin and her fellow plaintiffs alleged that the state of Ohio violated the ADA by failing to develop community-based services for the mentally disabled and hindering the expansion of such services in favor of institutional care—all at greater expense to the state. The state moved to dismiss the case, arguing the ADA did not require the creation of new Medicaid programs that would fund community setting care. But the plaintiffs were not seeking a new program—just the modification of an existing one. After the court overruled the state's motion the case settled in 2004, and 1500 disabled people were moved from institutional care to community-based care.

Martin's case helped set the stage for Ohio's Recovery Requires a Community Act in 2013. Ironically, while passed by a Republican-dominated legislature, the name evokes memories of Hillary Clinton's "it takes a village" concept of child development. Ideologies aside, the theme in both is clear: community involvement makes the difference.

Between fiscal year 2014 and 2016, 2000 people with behavioral problems who want to live in the community will be transferred from nursing homes to community settings and receive the appropriate services to live independently. Most will receive help from HOME Choice, a program administered by the Ohio Department of Job and Family Services that helps the disabled and elderly move from institutional care to home and community-based settings.

To qualify, residents must be eligible for Medicaid and require nursing home-type care that can be provided in a community setting. The cost must be no more than 80 percent of what Medicaid would pay for nursing home care.

The nursing home industry responded by lobbying for a pilot project in which 1000 current nursing home residents with behavioral problems would receive treatment at an enhanced payment rate. Presumably these individuals would have received enhanced treatment. The Kasich administration balked at the idea, according to Kirkman, and so the pilot project was converted into a study to develop recommendations for a pilot project.

"Funding a study to develop a pilot project is a big step backwards," says Kirkman. "We already know that many people with disabilities fare much better in the community than they do in an institutional setting, and helping these people live in the community costs the state less. What's left to study?"

Had she not passed a few years back, Nancy Martin would have agreed.

[The version published by *The Blade* was slightly shorter.]

Why has state fought compensating Johnston
July 16, 2017, Columbus Dispatch

If you believe the court system always renders justice, you're mistaken. Just ask Dale Johnston. After spending nearly seven years on Death Row for two murders he didn't commit, Johnston has yet to succeed in a 24-year ordeal to obtain compensation for his wrongful conviction.

And the real killer is now behind bars. Johnston was convicted in 1984 of killing his stepdaughter, Margaret Cooper, and her fiancée, Todd Schultz. The bodies were found nude, dismembered and decomposing. Each had been shot several times. Johnston's link to the murders was circumstantial evidence. After a series of appeals, Johnston was released from Death Row in 1990.

With freedom in hand, Johnston pursued a claim against the state. To prevail under the wrongful imprisonment statute, Johnston had to prove he had not committed the murders, but he failed to provide adequate proof, and his case was dismissed in 1993.

The statute was amended in 2003. Now, a wrongfully imprisoned individual could prove either actual innocence or the existence of a procedural error. Johnston filed a second action in 2008, alleging both. That same year, Charles McKnight pled guilty to murdering Cooper and Schultz.
For reasons not clear, Johnston dismissed his suit in 2010 and later re-filed. In 2012, the trial court granted

judgment in his favor. Quoting a U.S. Supreme Court case, the trial court held, "'The law knows no finer hour than when it cuts through formal concepts and transitory emotions to protect unpopular citizens against discrimination and persecution.'

In its wisdom, the General Assembly provided a remedial law for situations like this one, in which a citizen had been wrongfully convicted and imprisoned by errors of Constitutional significance. Mr. Johnston has shown he is entitled to relief."

The state appealed, and the Franklin County Court of Appeals held in 2014 that the amendment to the statute could not be applied retroactively to Johnson's case and reversed. Johnston appealed to the Ohio Supreme Court. The court held the amendment could be applied retroactively and sent the case back to the court of appeals.

Obligated on its second review to apply the amendment to Johnston's case, this time the court of appeals held that Johnston's case didn't meet the requirements of the amendment. With that, Johnston was down to his last move. He asked the Ohio Supreme Court in 2016 to review his case. On June 21, the court announced it would not hear the case.

How is it that an innocent man could be denied compensation for seven years on Death Row? Why in the world did Attorney General Mike DeWine feel compelled to appeal the trial court ruling in 2012?

Certainly, it was not the amount of money at stake. The state's exposure was $280,000 or so for the time Johnston spent on Death Row and whatever income he lost during that time and his attorney fees.

If DeWine was concerned about the precedent set by the trial court's ruling, he could have negotiated an out-of-court settlement in exchange for Johnston asking the trial court to vacate its ruling. How is it no one in DeWine's office thought about the big picture and fairness—Johnston deserved something for the seven years the state cost him.

Ohio Supreme Court Justice Paul E. Pfeifer was not impressed with the state's position. He asked during oral argument, "Why didn't the state just suck it up and say, 'Look, the prosecution of this thing was drop dead wrong. The investigation of it was wrong. It was a mess. It was a miscarriage of justice, Mr. Johnston.' So pay up. The state could have ended it right there."

What about the court of appeals? Couldn't it have seen things just a little differently so that Johnston could obtain some relief for what he endured. One of the three judges on the court's panel dissented and would have held in Johnston's favor.

Johnston had one last glimmer of hope. Rep. Bill Seitz, R-Cincinnati, proposed an amendment to the state budget bill, House Bill 49, that would fix what he contends are errors where the Ohio Supreme Court has "gone off the rails."

The amendment was opposed by DeWine, who is concerned it would provide financial compensation for those who are released from prison because of procedural errors, not innocence. Maybe DeWine has a point. Then again, perhaps the state should be held accountable, even when a person released from prison for procedural errors might be guilty. That's the price of violating constitutional safeguards.

Seitz's amendment was deleted from the final version of the budget that was just passed. His office stated the amendment will be introduced again as stand alone bill after the General Assembly's summer recess.

To someone like Dale Johnston, all this is mumbo-jumbo. All he knows is, the system has failed him.

Ex-offenders need a second chance
March 6, 2018, Columbus Dispatch

In his State of the Union address, President Donald Trump said the goal of lifting citizens "from poverty to prosperity" must "must be extended to all citizens … reforming our prisons to help former inmates who have served their time get a second chance." Trump didn't provide any details, but he touched on a huge problem.

The National Employment Law Project estimates 70 million Americans have been arrested or incarcerated. The Ohio Justice and Policy Center calculates nearly 2 million Ohioans have criminal convictions.

Finding employment is a significant challenge for ex-offenders, and stable employment, says Berkeley University professor Steven Raphael, is central to successful reentry into society. In Raphael's words, a criminal record is a modern day scarlet letter. Academic Devah Pager has concluded a criminal record reduces the chance of an employer call back by 50%.

Limited help is available in Ohio. Except for sexual or violent crimes, criminal records may be sealed by court order, and when a record is sealed, a conviction is "considered not to have occurred." But eligibility is limited. An offender cannot have more than two convictions and must wait three years after final discharge for a felony and one year for a misdemeanor to apply for relief.

In 2012, Ohio passed legislation to overcome licensing barriers. A theft conviction, for example, is a bar to obtaining a license to drive a school bus, and a drug offense is a bar to obtaining a teacher's license. By applying to a state court, an ex-offender may obtain a certificate of qualification for employment (CQE) that will remove several licensing impediments. But the process isn't available until six months after a misdemeanor sentence ends or one year after a felony sentence. Plus, the process is lengthy and somewhat difficult.

To address employer concerns about allegations of negligence in hiring an ex-offender, CQEs provide immunity. Results have been encouraging. In a study published in 2016, job applicants with a one-year-old felony conviction and a CQE did nearly as well as applicants with no criminal record in getting an interview or job offer and significantly better than applicants with a felony conviction and no CQE.

But CQEs don't solve the problem. From 2013 through 2016, only 3803 applications were submitted—20,000 people are released annually from Ohio prisons—and only 588 CQEs were granted. In Franklin County, 88 applications have resulted in 9 CQEs.

Ohio passed "ban the box" legislation in 2015 that prohibits questions on job applications about criminal background—but only for public employers. Sen. Sandra R. Williams (D-Cleveland) has proposed S.B. 49 that would do the same for the private sector. Introduced in

Feb. 2017, the bill has moved at glacial speed. Its first hearing was conducted last November, and there's no word about a second hearing.

One problem, says Court of Common Pleas Judge Richard A. Frye is that "judges have no discretion in sealing records for ex-offenders with multiple convictions, no matter how old the crime or how rehabilitated the applicant." Regarding the low number of CQE applications, Frye believes the process is too confusing and suspects most ex-offenders don't believe a judge will grant the CQE.

S.B. 66 seeks to increase eligibility for sealing records by eliminating limits on fourth and fifth degree felonies, but that's a modest improvement. "If the legislature really wants to help ex-offenders," says Frye, "it should broaden the window of eligibility for sealing records beyond its current, narrow confines."

Gary Mohr, Director of the Department of Rehabilitation and Correction, agrees. "Critical to reducing recidivism is reducing barriers to employment. I'd like to see judges have more discretion in sealing records. After people serve their sentence and show they deserve a second chance, we have to give it to them."

"If we don't, Mohr says, "it lands up costing society more in the long run."

What's the best way to measure patriotism?
June 22, 2018, Columbus Dispatch

We're in the midst of a national kerfuffle over what it means to be patriotic, and it has a lot more to do with ego and attitude than substance. Funny thing is, the man who started the ruckus never served in the military.

President Donald Trump has castigated NFL players for not standing during the national anthem and criticized franchise owners for allowing them to do so. Last week, he used the NBA finals to renew his spat with players LeBron James and Steph Curry—both had taken issue with his hard-line attitude—and said that neither the Warriors nor the Cavaliers would be invited to the White House.

Never heralded for consistency, Trump talks about showing respect for the military, but during his campaign he denigrated Sen. John McCain for being taken prisoner during the Vietnam War—as if it were McCain's fault he was shot down while flying combat over North Vietnam. As if Trump knows anything about combat.

Patriotism is easier to define than talk about in a meaningful way. The Oxford dictionary defines it as "devotion to and vigorous support for one's country." Nothing there about standing for the anthem. Outside of singing the anthem or serving in the military, how do you show devotion for your country?

If you repeatedly dodged the draft during the Vietnam War because of a bone spur in your foot, but you now criticize NFL franchise owners for allowing their players to take a knee during the anthem—are you patriotic? (Hello, President Trump.) Are you unpatriotic if you went to Canada during the Vietnam War but later returned to the U.S. and now teach in an inner-city public school where most students come from low-income families?

What if you never stand for or sing the anthem, but you mentor a fatherless child—are you less devoted to the U.S. than the guy who enthusiastically sings the anthem but cheats on his taxes? How about if you stand at attention for the anthem at weekend football games, but during the week you direct your employees to dump toxic waste into a nearby river—are you devoted to your country?

Just talking about whether the anthem should be part of sports events gets people lathered up. Columbus Dispatch sports writer Rob Oller questioned why the national anthem is sung at sporting events. He didn't criticize the anthem, and he didn't advocate taking a knee during the anthem to protest social wrongs. He simply questioned the connection between the anthem and sports.

Based on the reactions that followed, you would have thought Oller had advocated anarchy and flag burning. Readers referred to him as "disrespectful," said his column was an "affront" to patriotism, and called his

writing "ridiculous commentary." All this over a song.
As if the anthem alone defines patriotism.

Let's look at patriotism from a different angle. Criminal
defense attorney, Diane Menashe, has handled some 30
capital cases. Her work is thankless. Menashe's clients—
those accused of murder—are anything but sympathetic.
Most recently, she defended convicted sex offender
Brian L. Golsby who brutalized and murdered Ohio
State University student Reagan Tokes.

The average citizen probably doesn't understand why
Menashe handles these cases. But her work is critical.
Lawyers like Menasche ensure the government has to
proves its case and that defendants are not imprisoned
without the benefit of due process. Is Menashe just a
zealot, or is she demonstrating devotion to the
Constitution and the freedoms we all hold dear?

At his inauguration speech in 1961, President John F.
Kennedy gave us a sense of what patriotism is without
trying to define the term. "And so, my fellow
Americans: ask not what your country can do for you —
ask what you can do for your country."

Patriotism isn't what we say or whether we stand to sing
the anthem. If you measure patriotism by that standard,
then you've opted for a dollar store version of
patriotism. It's what we do for the nation that counts.
Let's have more doing and less talking.

Men are no more at risk now than before
October 17, 2018, The Columbus Dispatch

President Donald Trump warns that the Senate confirmation hearing for Brett Kavanaugh indicate that "it's a very scary time for young men in America." Fox journalist Jeanine Pirro believes the left is setting a new standard—"You are guilty until proven innocent"—and that due process, probable cause and reasonable doubt no longer have any meaning.

Let's drop the hyperbole and recognize that the Kavanaugh hearing, while ugly, was, in essence, a job interview on a national scale. What should have been a dignified process denigrated into a fight because the people doing the hiring couldn't agree on what mattered more. Thrilled with Kavanaugh's conservative record, Republicans were unconcerned about the allegations made against him, and Democrats acted like juveniles to prevent another conservative from being seated on the high court.

Sounding an alarm about due process and probable cause being thrown out the window only adds to the acrimony. Those concepts still matter—but at trial.

Job interviews aren't bound by what can be proven. If an employer doesn't feel good about how a candidate interviews, even if those concerns aren't substantiated, he doesn't get the job. The only way for Republicans to steer around the questions concerning Kavanaugh's background was to conflate the confirmation process with a trial. Kavanaugh is innocent until proven guilty, they argued, and there's no corroborating evidence. Except it wasn't a trial.

More disturbing is the alarm voiced by columnist Jay Ambrose who warns that men are now at greater risk because the potential for baseless allegations has increased. Evidence is no longer needed to be found guilty of sexual abuse. All that is required these days is for a #MeToo feminist to say the victim is a victim.

Ambrose cites the story of Gregory Counts and VanDyke Perry, who, between them, were wrongfully incarcerated in New York for 36 years for a rape they did not commit. A horrible blunder, but it happened in 1991, well before #MeToo came along.

The problem with stories like this is not so much about women conjuring up stories—the basis for Counts and Perry being wrongfully convicted—but more about our judicial system being fallible. Wrongful convictions happen more than most would think.

A few years back, I met six men—Ricky Jackson, Kwanme Ajamu, Wiley Bridgeman, Joe D'Ambrosio, Derrick Jamison and Dale Johnston—who had spent a combined 173 years incarcerated in Ohio—some on Death Row—for murders they did not commit before their convictions were overturned.

Samuel R. Gross of the University of Michigan Law School, Barbara O'Brien of the Michigan State

University College of Law and two research professionals estimated in a study published in 2014 by the National Academy of Sciences that 4.1 percent of all death-sentenced defendants are wrongly convicted.

With all things human, there will always be error, including trials. Wrongful convictions happen because of eyewitness misidentification, unreliable forensic science, false confessions, government misconduct, snitches who lie, judicial error and bad lawyering.

Here's the point: for all these shortcomings, we don't stop prosecuting murder cases, and there's no reason to even think about backing down on holding men accountable for sexual abuse. Instead, let's always work on improving the system.

Ambrose is worried the #MeToo movement will devolve into zealotry which, he fears, can lead to "different kinds of abuses, societal unfairness, indecency, to a guillotine that may not literally cut off heads but can cut off fundamental human rights" for men. Haven't women suffered these same injustices for years?

The world is no more dangerous for men today than it was 50 years ago. Only womanizers need fear the #MeToo movement.

If a man drinks in moderation, is mindful of the company he keeps and avoids questionable situations, his risk of being unfairly accused of sexual abuse is no worse than the risk any man faces of being wrongfully accused of any crime. Maybe some men simply don't like the idea of being held accountable.

Funding food assistance is good public policy
January 19, 2019, Columbus Dispatch

The farm bill, which provides assistance to farmers and funds the Supplemental Nutrition Assistance Program, formerly known as food stamps, was passed in December with bipartisan support in the House and Senate. Though controversial, SNAP funding was not fundamentally changed. However, after signing the bill, President Donald Trump announced he wants to tighten restrictions.

SNAP is controversial because it's perceived as an entitlement conservatives want to cut. They overlook that SNAP helps promote good health by making up in part for the social and economic factors that contribute to poor health for people living in poverty. Based on a 2016 study published in the Journal of the American Medical Association, the average 40-year-old man in the poorest 1 percent of American men will die 15 years sooner than a man in the richest 1 percent.

The Center on Budget and Policy Priorities think tank supports SNAP because its participants have lower medical costs and better health outcomes than low-income nonparticipants. Columbus Public Health Commissioner Dr. Mysheika Roberts stated at a Mid-Ohio Food Bank event in October that food-insecure adults are at greater risk for diabetes and obesity and that many chronic diseases can be prevented or reduced through access to healthy foods.

A 2013 study published in the Advances in Nutrition
journal found that food insecurity is associated with
more children having fair or poor health, more
hospitalizations and developmental issues.

In 2017, 42 million Americans — including 15 percent
of Ohioans — received SNAP. Seventy percent are in
families with children, and more than 25 percent are in
families with seniors or disabilities, according to the
Center. Eligibility for a family of four to receive a $640
montly benefit is limited to those with gross yearly
income of S31,980 or less.

Access to food means better health, eligibility
requirements are stringent, and individual payments are
modest — what's not to like? Answer: Those payments
and related costs add up to about $65 billion annually,
and conservatives don't like that. The administration has
proposed new rules that narrow eligibility guidelines and
reduce benefits.

White House interim chief of staff Mick Mulvaney says
he's worried his unborn grandchildren will be strapped
with the deficit that comes with supporting programs
like SNAP. Funny, but he's not concerned about the
increased deficit caused by the December 2017 tax cut or
the hunger that confronts kids right now.

A survey conducted more than a year ago by Mid-Ohio
Food Bank illustrates that Ohioans have a broad variety
of views on SNAP. While the majority of respondents
favored food assistance, many share Mulvaney's

position and question the government's role in nutrition assistance. Further, some see SNAP as a source of abuse, but Forbes contributor Simon Constable concludes that only 0.9 percent of SNAP money is subject to fraud.

Roberts believes "It's time to start looking at SNAP through a new lens — as public-health policy and not as an entitlement program." Matt Habash, president of the Mid-Ohio Food Bank, goes one step further: "We need to stop confusing public-health policy with employment goals for the poor."

Habash is referring to the type of attitude voiced last month by U.S. Rep. Warren Davidson, R-Troy, who said that stiffening the rules for SNAP gives people "who are trapped in government dependency a helping hand transitioning back into full-time employment."

It's not clear what Davidson was saying. Does he mean that people prefer unemployment because of the modest amount of SNAP benefits they receive, or that by suddenly denying benefits to participants, they'll be able to just as quickly find jobs? Regardless, he didn't offer any evidence for either position.

Here's how Habash puts it: "If we want to promote more employment for people at this economic level, and we should, then let's offer them a sustainable wage that allows families to provide for their basic needs. By reducing SNAP eligibility, we accomplish only one thing with certainty — poor health for more people."

A neighborhood's resources determine future
of its children
February 4, 2020, The Columbus Dispatch

You can determine the opportunities a Franklin County
child will likely have by his neighborhood. Social
determinants like health, education and incarceration
rates are indicators for success and portend a bleak
future for many neighborhoods. What's to be done?
First, let's look at the numbers.

If you live in Upper Arlington, your life expectancy is 82
to 84 years, according to the Kirwin Institute at The
Ohio State University. For someone in southern
Franklinton, it's 64 to 71 years, and nearly half of your
neighbors live at the poverty level ($25,750 for a family
of four). If you live in southern Columbus, the Centers
for Disease Control tell us you have a roughly 10 percent
chance of suffering from heart disease; the rate is about
2 percent in the northwest part of town.

Ten percent of Franklin County residents do not have a
high school diploma or GED. For South Linden, it's 26
percent. The incarceration rate for Franklin County is
three percent, while it's nearly 17 percent for South
Linden.

These statistics correlate with an opportunity index the
Ohio House Financing Agency has developed. The
county's northwest quadrant rates a very high
opportunity index. The southeast ranks mostly low and
very low.

HUD Secretary Ben Carson says that personal success is based on a "state of mind." Sounds simple enough, but how do you create that "state of mind" when your neighborhood is blighted?

A study funded by the CDC and two foundations concluded that nine steps, when implemented together—ranging from increasing employment opportunities to investing in high quality childcare and early education—will reduce poverty. All great ideas, but effecting change on this level is a tall order.

The Franklin County commissioners launched a blueprint last June with 120 recommendations for reducing poverty with goals of increased employment and higher paying jobs, more job training and greater academic success. Affordable housing is also part of the plan.

Bravo! But all this takes time, and much of the blueprint is in its initial state of planning stage and subject to the sway of politics. Historically, tax cuts for the wealthy and incentives for big business are what readily appeal to legislators.

A local initiative, Move to Prosper, has formed its own strategy, based on Maslow's hierarch of needs. Before self-actualization can happen, physical needs, such as food and shelter, and safety needs, such as personal security and employment, must be met. If these basic needs aren't met, individuals can't progress.

Loosely translated: if it's too hard to improve a neighborhood, then find a better one. Think about it—that's what people of means do. A study published in 2016 in the American Economic Review confirms the importance of neighborhood in a child's development, as does a study published this year by the Heller School for Social Policy and Management at Brandeis University.

Move to Prosper helps single mothers, who earn 50 percent of the county's median income and have one to three children, all under 13 years of age, move from neighborhoods with high poverty rates to neighborhoods with low crime rates, better housing and better performing schools. The program provides life coaching, limited assistance with rent, and goal setting.

It's a small operation and still in its infancy, but the results are promising. After four months in the pilot program, the nine participants were interviewed. Eight reported being better off financially and improved mental health, seven saw improvements in their children's behavior, and five saw improvements in their children's health.

As one mother put it, "This is changing our life. It's helping us get on our feet and giving us tools to maintain that life."

Project facilitator Amy Klaben and her steering committee want to grow the program to 100 women. "We're proving that lifting families out of poverty requires a comprehensive approach, and we've got a formula that works."

The Problems with Judicial Elections

There's a better way to get better judges
August 14, 2013, The Columbus Dispatch

In an op-ed piece published in May, Ohio Supreme
Court Chief Justice Maureen O'Connor concluded that,
based on a poll, "there is widespread agreement that we
should elect our judges." Believing it futile to advocate
merit appointment but seeing some change as necessary,
she has proposed eight changes to the judicial election
system. In a piece published on July 13, 2013, attorney
Bret A. Adams bitterly criticized judicial elections for
producing incompetent judges.

So, what's really going on? First, let's look at the
December 2012 Quinnipiac University poll to which
O'Connor refers. Here's the question that was asked:
"Which do you prefer: A) Keeping the current system of
electing Ohio Supreme Court judges; or, B) Changing to
a system in which new judges would be appointed by the
governor and confirmed by the legislature?"

Eighty-one percent of respondents preferred the current
system. This shouldn't come as a surprise. Four months
before, according to Public Policy Polling, Gov. John
Kasich's approval rating was only 41 percent. Who
wants a governor (much less an unpopular one at the
time) to control the judiciary?

The Quinnipiac poll speaks only to the public's dim
view of giving politicians more authority but says
nothing about what kind of judges voters want. We
should be investigating how the public would respond to

a system that would provide a higher likelihood of more qualified and competent judges.

The Ohio State Bar Association supports merit appointment with retention elections. The system is based on stated minimum qualifications, where candidates are screened by non-partisan committees and are judged on experience, skill and ability. Appointed judges would be subject to retention elections at regular intervals.

Adams is correct. The current system is not designed to produce good judges. In selecting judicial candidates, party bosses do the public a disservice. Their goal—who can get elected based on simple name recognition—is at odds with what the public needs in its judges—superior intellect, sound judgment, calm temperament, solid work ethic.

It's easy to infer from Adams' letter that the election system has produced mostly incompetent judges. True, we have some judges who perform poorly, but somehow, despite the parties' skewed priorities, we have many good judges. Still, we should do much better.

If Ohio's lawyers favor merit appointment, why doesn't the idea take hold? Simple. Its proponents are intimidated by the recent Quinnipiac poll and a referendum from nearly 30 years ago concerning merit appointment that failed. Apparently, no one feels the time is right to push the idea.

In their 2003 study, *Judicial Selection in Ohio,* authors Michael E. Solimine, Carolyn Chavez, Thomas Pulley, and Lee Sprouse tell the story of what happened with the 1987 referendum. The OSBA, Ohio League of Women Voters, and insurance and business communities joined forces to promote a ballot proposal for a merit selection system, known as Issue 3.

Issue 3 called for establishing nominating commissions for the supreme court and each of the courts of appeals. Each commission, composed equally of lawyers and non-lawyers, would screen candidates and propose three names to the governor, who would appoint one person. Once appointed, a judge would be required to face regular retention elections and receive at least a 55 percent approval vote to stay in office.

The unions and political parties opposed Issue 3, asserting it was elitist and anti-democratic and deprived Ohioans of the right to vote. Voters rejected Issue 3 approximately two to one. Solimine and his colleagues attribute its defeat to the effectiveness of the opponents' "right to vote" campaign. Apparently, the opponents were able to distract voters from the fact that retention elections were part of Issue 3.

Naysayers will argue that merit appointment will be subject to political forces, just as elections are, but in a less obvious way. Regardless of their criticism, we know this with certainty: the current system does nothing to ensure that the best candidates become judges.

O'Connor's proposals make sense if you agre
e that judicial elections are here to stay. But here's the
problem; at best, her proposals tepidly improve a bad
system.

We can do better, but changing the system requires that
we educate the public. It will be hard work, but nothing
worthwhile comes easily. The bar association and the
Supreme Court should embrace the idea of advancing
merit appointment with the legislature and reassuring
voters that, by virtue of retention elections, they will
retain the right to vote.

Judicial elections: a broken system (part 1)
Summer 2015, Columbus Bar Association Lawyers Quarterly

We have come to the point where we need to examine the practicality of judicial elections. Name recognition has become more important than qualifications, and the potential increases for politics and money to have a greater role and negative impact in judicial elections. Some think we need to amend the process by which we elect judges. I think the problems are too numerous to be fixed. It's time to give serious consideration to a merit appointment/retention election system.

Here are the three reasons why we need to change. Look for additional reasons in part two of this article, to be published in the next edition of Lawyers Quarterly.

1. The parties care more about name recognition <u>and fund raising ability than qualifications.</u>

Admittedly, my experience is limited to Franklin County, but I suspect that what happens here is typical of what goes on throughout the state. That point aside, the first problem with judicial elections is that they are controlled by the parties, and qualifications are not a high priority for the parties. The two most important things for a candidate are an ability to raise money and a likelihood of being elected (which usually means having a recognizable name.)

I understand from a friend who screened for a common pleas court seat in last November's election that the first question asked was, "How much money can you raise?" There was little discussion about qualifications.

There is a big disconnect between what the parties and practicing lawyers want. The Columbus Bar Association evaluates candidates on their qualifications and rates them as either "highly recommended," "acceptable" or "not recommended," but the CBA can only vet candidates who have been endorsed by the parties.

If the parties were concerned about qualifications, then every judicial candidate running in a Franklin County election would be rated "highly recommended" by the CBA, but that doesn't happen. In last November's elections, three trial judge candidates endorsed by the two major parties—plus a sitting trial judge—were only rated "acceptable." Two candidates—one for the appellate and one for the trial court—were actually "not recommended" by the CBA.[11] The incumbent trial judge was appointed by Gov. John Kasich over a much more experienced trial lawyer. If qualifications matter, why would that have happened?

Yes, the CBA vetting system is subjective and, therefore, subject to error, but it's an honest attempt to rate candidates on their qualifications. Besides, aren't

---

[11]http://www.cbalaw.org/cba_prod/files/polls/2014%20Judiciary%2 0Committee%20Findings.pdf (accessed Jan. 7, 2015).

lawyers are in the best position to determine who will make good judges?

What's worse, the parties make deals as to who they will run, to the detriment of voters. For example, in 2008, the Democratic Party agreed not to run candidates against three incumbent Republican judges in exchange for the Republican Party not running anyone against incumbent Democrat Judge Tim Horton.[12] A study conducted years earlier confirmed that the parties make these deals.[13] How do unopposed candidates serve the public good?

2. Names matter more than anything
    in judicial elections.

To illustrate the importance of names, let's look at one race in particular from last November and compare the candidates, who I'll refer to as Candidates A and B. Before going further, I have to tell you, Candidate A is a good friend and someone I think highly of. I have never met Candidate B but assume he is a good lawyer, a good person, and a hard worker.

Candidate A has been practicing law since 1987. He has tried over a hundred jury trials in a variety of civil cases, received the "Respected Advocate Award" from the

---

[12] Harmon, *Judge Horton Might Never Face Voters*, The Columbus Dispatch (June 16, 2009).

[13] Solimine, Chavez, Pulley & Sprouse, *Judicial Selection in Ohio: History, Recent Developments, and an Analysis of Reform Proposals*, Report of the Center for Law and Justice, University of Cincinnati College of Law (2003) at p. 24.

Ohio Association of Civil Trial Attorneys in 2011, and regularly serves as a mediator. Candidate B has been practicing law since 2005 and has tried 30 felony cases. The CBA "highly recommended" Candidate A. Candidate B was rated as "acceptable."

Based on these qualifications, you would assume Candidate A won, but that's not what happened. Candidate B won, and it's likely he won because of something that was given to him: a common last name that resonates with voters who have no other basis upon which to vote.

I don't mean to be critical of Candidate B. My focus here is not about people but about the process.

The problem with judicial races being determined on the basis of last names is hardly a newsflash. Plenty has been written about the name game in judicial races. Voters in Cuyahoga County are attracted to names such as Corrigan, Gallagher, McMonagle, Russo and Sweeney. [14] The name Cook works well in Summit County.[15] In Franklin County, names like O'Neill, Kennedy and Brown draw voters like a moth to flame.

---

[14] "The name game still vanquishes all else in Cuyahoga County judicial elections," Cleveland Plain Dealer (Sept. 05, 2014).
[15] "When electing judges, it's justice in name only," Akron Beacon Journal (Oct.15, 2014).

3. We should not conclude the public is
    adamant about voting for judges.

The 1987 referendum in which Ohioans rejected an
appointment/retention election system is regarded as
conclusive proof the public will reject change. I don't
think this nearly three-decade-old referendum fairly
reflects how voters feel today. Before I explain why,
let's look at what happened in the referendum.

The OSBA, the Ohio League of Women Voters, and the
insurance and business communities promoted a ballot
proposal for an appointment/retention election selection
system, known as Issue 3, which called for establishing
nominating commissions for the Supreme Court and
each appellate court. Each commission, composed
equally of lawyers and non-lawyers, would screen
candidates and propose three names to the governor for
appointment. Once appointed, a judge would be required
to receive at least a 55 percent approval vote in regular
retention elections to stay in office.[16]

The unions and political parties opposed Issue 3, casting
it as anti-democratic and elitist. They preyed on voters'
fears and claimed the commissions and governor would
be less attuned to the interests of the common person.[17]
They ran television ads that featured voting booths
encircled by chains and the sound bite, "Don't let them

---

[16] Solimine, Chavez, Pulley & Sprouse at 10.
[17] *Ibid.*

take away your right to vote."[18] The scare tactics were
successful. Issue 3 was soundly defeated.

More recently, Quinnipiac University conducted a poll
in Ohio and asked: "Which do you prefer: A) Keeping
the current system of electing Ohio Supreme Court
judges; or, B) Changing to a system in which new judges
would be appointed by the governor and confirmed by
the legislature?"[19]

Eighty-one percent of respondents preferred the current
system, which should not be surprising, considering that
Kasich's approval rating was just 41 percent four months
prior.[20] Who wants a governor (much less an unpopular
one at the time) to control the judiciary?

What voters say in response to polls and how they
conduct themselves, however, are two different things.
Voters may say they want to retain the right to vote for
judges, but many don't exercise that right. According to
the League of Women Voters, 40 percent of voters in
Ohio's November 2012 elections did not vote for
judges.[21] In the 2014 Ohio Judicial Election Survey,

---

[18] Jacob H. Huebert, "Judicial Elections and Their Opponents in
Ohio," The Federalist Society for Law & Public Policy Studies
(2010) at 12.
[19] http://www.quinnipiac.edu/news-and-events/quinnipiac-
university-poll/ohio/release-detail?ReleaseID=1823 (accessed Jan.
7, 2014).
[20] *Ibid*; "Kasich approval on the rise," Public Policy Polling (Aug.
15, 2012).
[21] http://www.lwvohio.org/site.cfm/Voter-Election-Center/Judicial-
Voter-Information.cfm (accessed April 3, 2015.)

conducted by the Ray C. Bliss Institute of Applied Politics, University of Akron, 30 percent of respondents stated they voted for judges "most" or about "half the time;" 20 percent said "not very often," "rarely," or "never."[22]

When responding to a referendum or poll about voting rights, people are dealing with a question in the abstract, but when you *talk with people* about how they feel about the system, you hear something quite different. I've talked to a number of non-lawyers about judicial elections, and I hear cries of frustration. Voters don't know who they should vote for, and the reason is, they don't have meaningful information about the candidates.

Ask your friends how they feel about voting for judges. Even lawyers who don't litigate will tell you they don't have enough information when voting for judges— unless they ask their litigator friends for help. I think people are ready for change.

---

[22] https://www.uakron.edu/dotAsset/f1ab548d-8b9d-40cd-ab0a-844236cb7a0d.pdf (accessed April 3, 2015.)

Judicial elections: a broken system (part 2)
Fall 2015, Columbus Bar Association Lawyers Quarterly

In the first installment of this article, I dealt with two issues that make elections unworkable in judicial elections—the political parties' lack of concern for a candidate's qualification, and voter reliance on name recognition. I also reviewed a third issue, the failed 1987 referendum which would have put into place an appointment/retention election system, and a 2010 poll. Here are the fourth and fifth reasons why the system is broken.

4.   Judicial Races might become more political.

In 2002, the U.S. Supreme Court held in *Republican Party of Minnesota v. White*[23] that judicial candidates cannot be precluded from stating their views on legal issues. The case concerned the state's Code of Judicial Conduct, which prohibited both judges and candidates from announcing their views on disputed legal and political issues. The court found the clause to be unconstitutional.

Based on *White*, Ohio's Code of Judicial Conduct may be subject to attack. As it stands, Ohio judges and candidates are prohibited from making "any statement that would reasonably be expected to affect the outcome or impair the fairness of a matter pending or impending

---

[23] 536 U.S. 765, 122 S. Ct. 2528 (2002)

in any court." Judges and candidates are also prohibited from making committing themselves to positions in connection with cases or issues that are likely to come before the court that are "inconsistent with the impartial performance of the adjudicative duties of judicial office."[24]

Is the purpose of the Ohio Code to ensure that judges and candidates will be impartial? If so, this goal has already failed to impress the U.S. Supreme Court: "A judge's lack of predisposition regarding the relevant legal issues in a case has never been thought a necessary component of equal justice, and with good reason. For one thing, it is virtually impossible to find a judge who does not have preconceptions about the law."[25] Moreover, "there is almost no legal or political issue that is unlikely to come before a judge of an American court, state or federal, of general jurisdiction."[26]

When running for the Ohio Supreme Court in 2002, then-Hamilton County Municipal Judge Tim Black referred to the seat vacated by Justice Andrew Douglas as "labor's seat."[27] This freely expressed political opinion came just months after *White* was decided. We have not seen many candidates taking advantage of the freedoms that comes with the *White* decision, but that

---

[24] Ohio Code of Judicial Conduct, Rule 4.1(A)(6) and (7)

[25] 536 U.S. at 777

[26] 536 U.S. at 772

[27] "Justice hopefuls: Don't assume" www.enquirer.com/editions/2002/09/23/loc_justice_hopefuls.html (Sept. 23, 2002).

might be attributed to the reticence on the part of candidates.

The Ohio Code of Judicial Conduct was modified in March 2009 to allow judicial candidates to state their political affiliation at any time. Previously, judges could identify their political affiliation only until the primaries ended.[28] The Court of Appeals for the Sixth Circuit in *Carey v. Wolnitzek* struck down as unconstitutional Kentucky's judicial canons that prohibited judicial candidates from identifying themselves as members of a political party.[29]

In 2014, judicial candidates were given somewhat more leeway in campaigning. Based on the holding from *In Re Judicial Campaign Complaint Against O'Toole* that part of Jud.Cond.R. 4.3(A) violates the First Amendment, the rule has been amended.[30]

The rule previously read as follows:

> During the course of any campaign for nomination or election to judicial office, a judicial candidate *** shall not knowingly or with reckless disregard do any of the following:

---

[28] Compare Jud.Cond.R. 4.2(C)(6), with Canon 7(B) in the prior code.
[29] 614 F.3d 189, 204 (6th Cir. 2010).
[30] 141 Ohio St.3d 355, 2014-Ohio-4046

(A) Post, publish, broadcast *** information
concerning the judicial candidate or an opponent,
either knowing the information to be false or
with a reckless disregard of whether or not it was
false or, if true, that would be deceiving or
misleading to a reasonable person.

The last 13 words in Rule 4.3 (A)—"or, if true, that
would be deceiving or misleading to a reasonable
person"—have been eliminated.

Advocates of elections will argue that greater freedom in
campaigning will help voters be better informed.
Perhaps this is true, but greater freedom in voicing
opinions during elections brings about some troubling
consequences. Judges and judicial candidates may
become recognized more for the positions they advocate
than for their ability to competently handle the work of
judges. As candidates become vocal on their positions,
judicial elections could become more of a forum for how
judges should be deciding issues, and the matter of
judicial qualification would further diminish.

5. Money has no place in judicial election,
    but it's there.

In last November's Ohio Supreme Court elections,
common pleas court Judge John P. O'Donnell accused
Justice Judi French of "pocketing" campaign
contributions from American Electric Power and being

in "in the pocket of big utilities."[31] O'Donnell was referring to a case before the Ohio Supreme Court—and AEP's campaign contributions to Justice French—where the court ruled that AEP could retain some $368 million in charges that were questioned by consumers. Was this a cheap shot? Yes. Could money take on a bigger role in public perception of the Ohio Supreme Court and the practice of law before the court? Absolutely.

The U.S. Supreme Court's 2009 decision in *Caperton v. A.T. Massey Coal Co., Inc.*[32] paves the way, and the facts in that case are disturbing. After a $50 million verdict was rendered against A.T. Massey Coal, its CEO, Don Blankenship, decided that to prevail on appeal, he had to change the composition of the West Virginia Supreme Court.[33] He did this by supporting Brent Benjamin against incumbent Chief Justice Warner McGraw.

Blankenship contributed $2.5 million to "And For The Sake Of The Kids," a political action committee that characterized McGraw as too soft on crime and too dangerous for kids, and spent half a million on advertising. Altogether, Blankenship alone spent three times what Benjamin's own committee spent. A year before Massey's case came before the court, Benjamin was seated as its new chief justice. Caperton asked Benjamin to recuse himself, but he declined, and

---

[31] "O'Donnell finally hits TV with French attack ad," Columbus Dispatch (Oct. 26, 2014)

[32] 556 U.S. 868, 129 S.Ct. 2252, 173 L.Ed.2d 1208 (2009).

[33] West Virginia does not have an intermediate appellate court.

Caperton's case was dismissed by a 3-2 vote. You can probably guess who the swing vote was.

Caperton argued that Benjamin's failure to recuse himself violated the Due Process Clause of the Fourteenth Amendment. The U.S. Supreme Court agreed. In his dissent, Chief Justice Roberts stated that challenges based on the *Caperton* decision will "bring our judicial system into undeserved disrepute, and diminish the confidence of the American people in the fairness and integrity of their courts."[34] I'm not sure Chief Justice Roberts has it right. Are we to stay silent about a critical issue—the possibility of money influencing judges, which already creates the appearance of impropriety—so as to avoid scandal?

Asserting that the integrity of judges should be presumed ignores human nature. Twenty-seven state justices filed amicus briefs in support of Caperton's position, stating that financial support "can influence a judge's future decisions, both consciously and unconsciously."[35] After all, "every judge is first and foremost a human being, not a detached and unemotional law machine."[36]

In 2012, Ohio was among five states that had the most expensive state high court elections, with just under $3.5

---

[34] 556 U.S. at 902.

[35] Brief of Amicus Curiae 27 Former Chief Justices and Justices in Support of Petitioners at 5.

[36] *Id.* at 6.

million going to Supreme Court candidates.[37] Try explaining to the average American worker how $3.5 million in campaign funds don't influence candidates.

How do judicial candidates feel about this? Ask Ohio Supreme Court Justice Paul Pfeifer. Putting things in his own inimitable style: "I never felt so much like a hooker down by the bus station in any race I've ever been in as I did in a judicial race. Everyone interested in contributing has very specific interests."[38]

Regrettably, the fact is that studies show a strong correlation between campaign donations and decisions made by state high courts. A New York Times study found that Ohio Supreme Court Justices "routinely sat on cases after receiving campaign contributions from the parties involved or from groups that filed supporting briefs. On average, they voted in favor of contributors 70 percent of the time."[39] A study published by the American Constitution Society for Law and Policy made similar findings in all states where judges are elected.[40]

What precludes someone from duplicating in Ohio what Blankenship did in West Virginia? What precludes a

---

[37] "Do campaign donations in judicial races influence court decisions?" Stateline, The PEW Charitable Trusts (June 11, 2013)
[38] "Campaign cash mirrors a high court's ruling," New York Times (Oct. 1, 2006)
[39] *Ibid.*
[40] Joanna Shepherd, "Justice at risk, an empirical analysis of campaign contributions and judicial decisions," American Constitution Society for Law and Policy (June 2013)

litigant in Ohio from presenting a *Caperton*-type challenge? Are these scenarios we want to see in Ohio?

<u>Moving forward</u>. The threshold question is, how do most lawyers feel? I suspect most are concerned about the current state of judicial elections. If I'm right, then the next question is, what can be done?

The OSBA has favored an appointment/retention election system since 1987 but hasn't done much to promote change. I think it's time to inquire if the OSBA wants to take up the challenge.

Judges probably influenced by campaign money
July 30, 2017, The Columbus Dispatch

Do campaign contributions affect how judges decide cases? Studies indicate the answer is yes. A recent effort by Cleveland attorney Subodh Chandra to disqualify a Summit County judge illustrates how money might drive the public's thinking on a judge's impartiality.

First, some background. In 2009, the U.S. Supreme Court held in *Caperton v. A.T. Massey Coal Co.* that Chief Justice Brent Benjamin of the West Virginia Supreme Court erred in not recusing himself from a case concerning a $50 million judgement against Massey Coal. Massey's president had contributed $3 million to Benjamin's election campaign, and Benjamin was the swing vote in reversing the judgment.

In 2012, Ohio was among five states that had the most expensive state high court elections, with just under $3.5 million going to Ohio Supreme Court candidates.

In the 2014 Oho Supreme Court race, Cuyahoga County Judge John P. O'Donnell publicly criticized sitting Justice Judith French for accepting campaign contributions from utility executives and employees and then hearing a case concerning American Electric Power.

Let's get back to Attorney Chandra, who represents the plaintiffs in a class action suit against Kisling Nestico & Redick (KNR), a Cleveland law firm. The case was assigned to Summit County Judge Alison Breaux, newly elected in Nov. 2016. Suspecting Breaux was biased against his case—Chandra alleged she had shown a "hostile demeanor" and issued "plainly erroneous" decisions—Chandra investigated Breaux's campaign contributions.

Chandra learned that Breaux had received six months' free use of a billboard truck from KNR. She reported the value of her use of the truck at $3600. Valuations Chandra quoted from a political consulting firm and an advertising company put the value at $24,000 to $43,200. Breaux's campaign had received $93,000 in monetary contributions.

Chandra asserted that Breaux and Judge Joy Oldfield, who was also supported by KNR, "ran a joint campaign," meaning that a contribution to Oldfield was "effectively a contribution" to Breaux. By supporting Oldfield, KNR was able to support Breaux indirectly as well as directly.

Chandra asked the Ohio Supreme Court to disqualify Breaux, claiming she could not act impartially. Breaux responded, "I can unequivocally state that I am not biased against plaintiff or his counsel nor am I biased toward KNR." She denied suffering from "any bias, whatsoever, or impropriety which would cloud" her judgment.

Chief Justice Maureen O'Connor denied Chandra's request. "It is not reasonable to question a judge's impartiality based solely" on campaign contributions. She also found his statements to be speculative and insufficient to establish bias.

O'Connor's decision is not surprising. The bar to disqualifying a judge is high. Plus, to disqualify Breaux, O'Connor would have had to draw a line about campaign contributions in a system where practically every judge relies on them.

Breaux's reckoning of the situation misses the mark, which is also not surprising. People seldom admit to bias because it often operates on a subconscious level.

But studies that analyzed state supreme court decisions indicate that money influences judicial decisions. In her 2013 work, "Justice at Risk," Professor Joanna Shepherd of Emory University examined the explosion in campaign contributions for high court races across the union. Contributions skyrocketed from $83 million throughout the 1990s to $207 million from 2000 to 2009.

Shepard found "a statistically significant relationship between campaign contributions from business groups and justices' voting in favor of business interests." A justice who receives half his contributions from business groups, Shepard concluded, "would be expected to vote in favor of business interests almost two-thirds of the time."

In 2006, the *New York Times* published its study concerning Ohio Supreme Court justices. Ohio justices were found to have "voted in favor of contributors 70 percent of the time."

Perhaps we need to acknowledge that elected judges are politicians—at least to some extent, anyway. U.S. Supreme Court Chief Justice John Roberts may disagree—"Judges are not politicians, even when they come to the bench by way of the ballot"—but judges make campaign promises (usually limited to being tough on crime), glad hand and attend fundraisers to finance their campaigns.

Why should we expect judges not to be influenced—at least on some level—by the contributions they receive? Judges take the bench with all the foibles that are part of our humanity. To think otherwise is to ask far too much of a human being. Retired Supreme Court Justice Sandra Day O'Connor had it right: "A saint would be hard-pressed to disregard the fact that one litigant gave them a huge donation while the other gave nothing."

The role of money in judicial elections will only increase. At some point, a litigant will challenge one of Ohio's Supreme Court justices to recuse himself. Then do we finally examine whether the system should be changed?

Let's admit that state judges are politicians
November 18, 2020, The Columbus Dispatch

Let's admit it. Like it or not, state judges are politicians, and their party affiliation should be shown on general ballots, just like it is for every other politician.

Party affiliation is not disclosed on judicial ballots because we like the fiction that judicial races are nonpartisan and, perhaps we're even a little enamored of the idea that judges are above the political fray. It's a quaint notion that doesn't reflect today's reality.

We just saw bare-knuckled attack ads in two races. Appellate court judge Jennifer Brunner was criticized for supposedly putting children at risk because of an evidentiary ruling she made concerning a teacher accused of surreptitiously videoing underage girls undressing. Ohio Supreme Court Justices Judith French and Sharon Kennedy were said to be protecting rapists because of their rulings upholding the caps on damages available in civil rape cases.

We've seen this before. In 2000, an ad featuring the scales of justice filled with money announced that Ohio Supreme Court Justice Alice Robie Resnick received $750,000 in campaign contributions from trial lawyers and asked, "Is justice for sale in Ohio?"

Were all these messages taken out of context and in bad taste? Sure, but show me a political ad that is balanced

and truthful. Judges might not want to think of
themselves as politicians, but those in the messaging
business sure do.

The average voter has no clue about a judicial
candidate's qualifications, but one thing the average
voter does know is a candidate's political affiliation —
because the parties advertise their endorsements. Look at
what just happened in Franklin County. Democrats won
all 10 judicial races, even when running against
Republican incumbents.

Does job performance have anything to do with this?
Not likely. Republican Jenifer French lost her job, even
though the Columbus Bar Association gave her the third
highest rating among 17 common pleas court judges.
Veteran domestic court judge Dana Preisse, a
Republican, lost her seat, and she was highly rated.
Republican appellate court judge Lisa Sadler's very
favorable rating didn't help her keep her job.

Bottom line: if you want to serve as a judge in Franklin
County and you're a Republican, look for another line of
work.

It's no different for statewide judicial races. Republican
incumbent Kennedy held off Democrat challenger John
O'Donnell, a reflection of Ohioans voting Republican at
the top of the ballot. The exception was incumbent
Republican Justice French's loss to Democrat challenger
Jennifer Brunner. Neither has what are regarded as good
candidate names — O'Neill or Brown in Franklin

County; Corrigan or McMonagle in Cuyahoga — but Brunner's prior service as secretary of state might have made the difference.

Aren't Supreme Court justices obligated to disregard party affiliation when rendering decisions? Certainly, they are. "My job as a judge is to be an umpire, to call balls and strikes," French has stated. "It's not to bring my own personal biases into the cases in front of us. And that is that. There are times when I may not like the result at all." French's sentiment is noble, but party affiliation determines what strike zone a justice sees.

Justices might genuinely believe their party affiliation has nothing to do with how they vote, but that's conscious level thinking. Subconsciously, justices bring to the bench the same filters and biases we all have, and they generally subscribe to the policies advocated by their party.

Tell me a justice's political persuasion, and I can predict with reasonable certainty how she will decide a case.

Occasionally a notable exception comes along, such as retired Justice Paul Pfeifer, who was a liberal dressed in Republican clothes.

I've written plenty about the serious and many shortcomings of judicial elections and the advantages of a merit appointment system based on objective criteria. Until the day comes when we change the system — likely never, regrettably — judicial elections should at least reflect reality.

The Judicial System (and its shortcomings)

No one should go to court without counsel
February 19, 2013, The Columbus Dispatch

Fifty years ago, the U.S. Supreme Court decided in
Gideon v. Wainwright that indigent defendants must be
provided counsel in criminal cases. Still, the indigent
face significant hurdles when it comes to the legal
system.

Last July, I wrote about indigent defendants who can't
afford counsel in misdemeanor cases; unable to pay
court-ordered costs and fines, many are unlawfully jailed
by Ohio judges who don't understand the limits of their
authority. There's another problem as well. The indigent
are expected to make their way through complicated,
high-stakes civil cases, such as child custody or
Medicaid cases, without counsel.

The notion that justice and fair play are the birthright of
all citizens is something we assume to be true, but it
doesn't materialize for people who have to deal with the
legal system without counsel. "Without counsel in the
courtroom," says George Hausen, executive director of
Legal Aid of North Carolina, "the courthouse door
indeed is effectively closed and locked to poor litigants."
Unrepresented individuals who try to litigate custody
issues, defend against foreclosure actions or pursue
disability benefits are set up for failure.

Gideon's mandate is limited to cases where incarceration
is at stake, a point the U.S. Supreme Court confirmed in
1981 with *Lassiter v. Department of Social Services.* The

court held that a presumption exists "that an indigent litigant has a right to appointed counsel only when, if he loses, he may be deprived of his physical liberty. It is against this presumption that all the other elements in the due process decision must be measured."

Stated in simpler terms, rare is the civil case where an indigent defendant will be afforded court appointed counsel. In *Lassiter,* an indigent mother was denied court appointed counsel in an action the state initiated to terminate her parental rights.

Recognizing the problems the indigent face, the American Bar Association issued a resolution in 2006 that federal and state governments should "provide legal counsel as a matter of right at public expense to low-income persons in those categories of adversarial proceedings where basic human needs are at stake, such as those involving shelter, sustenance, safety, health or child custody." For these "high-stakes" proceedings, the ABA stated that the government should be obligated to ensure that low-income citizens have effective legal representation.

Several states have followed the ABA's lead. The Alaska and Pennsylvania state bar associations have passed similar resolutions. Hawaii, Maryland, Minnesota and other states have established commissions to study the degree to which the indigent are at risk. In 2009, California passed the Sargent Shriver Civil Counsel Act, which funded a six-year pilot project that provides counsel for indigent litigants in certain high-stakes cases.

Ohio has not gotten on board. Our state bar association has not passed a resolution that models the ABA resolution, nor has the state bar or the Ohio Supreme Court formed a commission to study the problem.

The future looks bleak in Ohio. Legal Aid offices, which provide assistance to people living below 125% of the Federal Poverty Level—just over $29,000 for a family of four—face decreasing federal funding, and interest rates on attorney trust accounts that fund Legal Aid have plummeted. Last month, Southeastern Ohio Legal Services closed three offices in Lancaster, Marietta, and Zanesville, which had served nine counties. The workload for those counties is being distributed among three other offices.

According to Jim Daniels, director for Southeastern Legal, his attorneys now provide representation only in the most serious cases. "We no longer provide representation in custody cases unless there is significant domestic violence for which we have special funding." Assistance in landlord-tenant issues is now limited to situations where a tenant has been kicked out, or his utilities have been turned off, or his possessions have been taken by a landlord.

Similar cutbacks have been made in other areas of the law affecting the poor. "For many," Daniels said, "the courts will now be hearing only one side of the story."

What's the answer? Expand funding for Legal Aid offices so that the indigent get a level playing field when it comes to high-stakes such as shelter, sustenance, safety, health or child custody. Private attorneys also need to lend a greater hand. "Accurate and just results are most likely to be obtained," Hausen maintains, "through the equal contest of opposed interests." That's what *Gideon* is all about.

Many indigent are unlawfully jailed
July 27, 2013, The Columbus Dispatch

True or false—debtors' prisons exist in the U.S.? Sadly, the answer is *true*, and debtors' prisons exist because the indigent often face misdemeanor charges without the benefit of counsel. Fifty years ago, the U.S. Supreme Court decided in *Gideon v. Wainwright* that indigent defendants in criminal cases must be provided with court-appointed counsel, but many Ohio counties do not provide counsel in misdemeanor cases where the court is trying to collect money.

As a consequence, the indigent are often imprisoned for their failure to pay fines and court costs. What's really disturbing is that many times these people are wrongfully incarcerated. The U.S. Supreme Court held in 1983 that it is unconstitutional to imprison people for not paying fines or court costs when they lack the financial means to pay. Imprisonment is permissible only after a court conducts a hearing concerning the person's financial condition and concludes that a person has willfully refused to pay.

By statute, this process must be followed in Ohio and, if imprisoned, a person must be credited $50 against the fine for every day of jail time. Imprisonment is never permissible for failing to pay court costs.

According to the American Civil Liberties Union of Ohio, from 1999 to 2011 the number of people living in poverty in Ohio increased by 58 percent. As poverty increases, more people are at risk for being wrongfully imprisoned.

In a report released last April, the ACLU found that in a six month period in 2012, nearly a quarter of the jail bookings in Huron County were related to failure to pay fines. According to the report, the staff at the Norwalk Municipal Court Clerk's Office in Huron County admitted that when court records show a person to have been incarcerated for 10 days on a contempt charge, the defendant was likely jailed for failure to pay fines. According to Ohio Public Defender Tim Young, "Because these people are not represented by counsel, they have no idea what their rights are. They just get pushed around."

ACLU observers reported that the typical process in the Norwalk Municipal Court is for a defendant to be found guilty of an offense and then ordered to pay fines and court costs by a certain date. If payment is not made, the court issues a summons requiring an appearance in court where the defendant is assigned a payment schedule.

Typically, no inquiry is made as to financial status and ability to pay. Defendants are not informed of their right to counsel and are warned that if they do not stay current with the payment plan, they will be required to turn themselves in to jail on a specific date.

If the defendant does not pay the amount due or report to jail on the appointed date, an arrest warrant is issued, and the defendant will be incarcerated for 10 days. This process results in additional fees, meaning that upon release, the defendant will find himself facing even more fees and the possibility of more jail time.

"Regrettably, several of these cases had to go up on appeal," said Young. "It's hard to believe this kind of abuse occurs, but it does." The ACLU found similar practices in the Hamilton County Municipal Court and the municipal courts in Bryan, Mansfield, Parma and Sandusky. Young agrees that the problem occurs in several areas in Ohio.

Tricia Metcalf's story, as related in an ACLU report, is typical. A single mother of two teens, Metcalf was convicted in 2006 of passing bad checks, which resulted in the imposition of a fine and a payment plan of $50 per month. Working minimum wage jobs, money was often tight. If she missed a payment, an arrest warrant was issued, and Metcalf would be incarcerated.

Metcalf once asked the judge about doing community service and extra time to pay. Some extra time was allowed, but she was eventually jailed. Since 2006, Metcalf has been incarcerated five times. The uncertainty of her situation hurt her ability to work and caused her children to move in with her mother. At one point, she owed $2000 and was jailed for 37 days. The court never conducted a hearing to evaluate her ability to pay.

Being represented by counsel would likely have made a difference for Metcalf, but Young explained that most counties can't afford public defenders for misdemeanor cases. Of course, one has to wonder how it is that we have judges who do not understand the limits of their authority, but that's a subject for another day.

So, here we are, 50 years after Gideon's mandate to fix the legal system, and still the indigent are being wrongfully imprisoned.

Drug courts can help reduce recidivism
August 20, 2014, The Columbus Dispatch

If we don't find a better way of dealing with non-violent drug offenders, we may find ourselves building more prisons. That's the concern of Gary C. Mohr, Director of the Department of Rehabilitation and Correction. We're good at putting drug offenders in jail, but we're not doing so well helping them with their addictions, which means they're likely to be repeat visitors at state prisons. That means more expense for the state and a loss of productivity in the economy.

This is a big problem that is growing. Mohr has seen Ohio's prison population skyrocket during his 40 year career. In 1974, Ohio housed 8500 inmates in state facilities. That number has grown to 50,500, nearly a six fold increase, while Ohio's population has grown by only eight percent to 11.5 million. Drug-related offenses are driving the increase in our prison population.

Ohio sent 20,120 individuals to state prisons in fiscal year 2014. For prison commitments in Ohio's six most populous counties (Cuyahoga, Franklin, Hamilton, Lucas, Montgomery, and Summit), 21.5 percent were for drug offenses, but the number was 30 percent for the other 82 counties. Of those offenders classified as truly non-violent—no prior arrests, indictments, or convictions for a violent offense—51 percent were incarcerated for drug offenses and are serving sentences of less than a year.

What to do? For starters, Mohr wants to change the way
we deal with non-violent drug offenders. "Conviction
does not end addiction," he says. "Prison has become the
default sanction for drug offenses, and prison programs
are not as effective in addressing addiction as are
community programs."

Mohr would like to see more "drug courts," where
judges have more options in sentencing, and serious
attention is given to rehabilitation. The process usually
begins after sentencing. If deemed to be an eligible
candidate for drug court—dealers and repeat offenders
do not qualify—the offender is given the option of
participating in a rehabilitation program in lieu of jail
time.

Drug court participants are placed on probation while
undergoing rehab and are regularly monitored. If they
deviate from the program, they are held accountable and
returned to the court. A drug court judge has tools at his
disposal to get an offender back on track, such as
ordering a few days in jail. Those who remain
noncompliant lose their probation status and serve their
sentences. If an offender successfully completes the
program, the charges brought against him are reduced or
dismissed.

A 2012 study in the *Journal of Criminal Justice*
indicates that drug courts are effective. The average
recidivism rate nationwide for non-drug court offenders
is 50 percent, but the drug courts that were studied had a
recidivism rate of 37 percent. Similar specialty courts for

drunk drivers had recidivism rates of 38 percent. Nationwide, the "graduation rate" for drug courts is just under 50 percent.

An evaluation completed in 2011 by the National Institute of Justice and other research groups concluded that drug court participants with violence histories had success rates comparable to those without violence histories. Drug court participants also reported less family conflict and were more likely than non-drug court contemporaries to be enrolled in school. They were also, on the whole, more self-reliant six months after completing their programs.

What makes drug courts successful? It's simple. They have leverage. The participants know exactly what they stand to lose if they break the rules. Participants are monitored and routinely appear before the same judge. While there is a written schedule of sanctions for violations, drug court judges have discretion in meting out sanctions and deftly employ both carrot and stick.

Ohio has 96 drug courts, the first one created in 1995, and eight specialty courts for drunk drivers. To put these numbers in perspective, Franklin County's municipal and common pleas court systems have 32 courts and two specialty courts for drugs.

To promote the idea that Ohio should be investing in people instead of prisons, Mohr convened a "best practices" round table in June, likely the first event of its kind for Ohio. Officials from nearly every county in

Ohio attended. Four of the speakers were judges who preside over courts for drunk drivers and drug offenders in Clermont, Hamilton, Hardin and Cuyahoga County.

Mohr believes that drug courts and community rehab programs have twice the success rate of jail programs. "The prison system isn't designed to be responsive to non-violent drug offenders. We have to always look for better solutions, and drug courts are a step in the right direction." There's the savings too. The NIJ reports that the reduction in recidivism rates and other long term costs result in savings of $6744 per participant.

Putting drug offenders in jail is easy. Doing what it takes to keep them from returning is the challenge.

State should support legal aid
May 27, 2018, The Columbus Dispatch

Is access to legal assistance for low-income Americans important? President Donald Trump doesn't think so. His 2018 budget proposed eliminating the Legal Services Corporation (LSC), an independent nonprofit, established during the Nixon administration that provides civil legal aid to low-income Americans.

Trump apparently forgot about his campaign theme—"to bring hope to every forgotten stretch of this country." According to former LSC president Martha Bergmark, the majority of the states with the lowest ranking for access to legal assistance for low-income citizens supported Trump.

Fortunately, most of Congress didn't listen to Trump. In fact, Congress went a different direction and increased LSC funding in March from $385 million to $410 million.

Across the country, legal aid offices serve the needs of those whose incomes are below 125 percent of the federal poverty level (FPL). For a family of four, that's $30,740 a year. Roughly 1.5 million Ohioans fall in this category. In 2016, the 28 lawyers and staff members at the Legal Aid Society of Columbus, along with several hundred pro bono attorneys and non-lawyer volunteers, served 6609 low-income individual and families.

It's probably difficult to imagine why those with low incomes would need a lawyer, but low income, in and of itself, generates problems. Seventy-one percent of low income households have experienced a legal problem in the past year. For households with disabled persons, the percentage jumps to 80 percent; for households with survivors of domestic violence or sexual assault, it jumps to 97 percent. One in four low-income households has experienced six or more legal problems in the past year.

"When living on the edge, one problem begets another," explains Tom Weeks, executive director of the Legal Aid Society of Columbus. "Get injured on the job without health insurance or workers compensation, and suddenly you're faced with hospital bills. Because you're unable to work, you can't afford to repay the auto title loan you took out for repair work, and you don't have money for next month's rent.

"You can afford to pay the lender or the landlord but not both. Eventually, the hospital files suit to collect on its unpaid bills. The lender and landlord will be next. It can be overwhelming."

What's staggering is that intimate partner violence among people with family income at or below the FPL is about four times the rate for those with incomes at or above 400 percent of the FPL. "Twenty-two percent of legal aid work is family law," says Angie Lloyd, executive director of the Ohio Legal Assistance Foundation. "But it's actually all domestic violence-related, so we're only meeting part of the domestic legal need."

Legal aid isn't just about providing assistance. "It's transformative work," says Lloyd, "that allows low-income and vulnerable Ohioans to be gainfully employed, financially secure, stably housed, healthy and safe from domestic violence."

The Access to Justice Task Force formed by Chief Justice Maureen O'Connor of the Ohio Supreme Court concluded there is a 115 percent return for every dollar invested in legal aid. "Studies consistently show that investing in civil legal aid programs has a positive economic impact."

Even if LSC funding continues in the future, it's not enough. LSC provides only roughly 30 percent of the budget for Ohio's legal aid offices. Another 40 percent comes from a surcharge on court filing fees and the interest earned on lawyer trust accounts, and that money has been decreasing. With interest rates dropping over the years, revenues from trust accounts fell from $22 million in 2007 to $4 million today.

Remarkably, the state of Ohio contributes nothing to legal aid. The Ohio Supreme Court's Task Force recommended in 2015 that the Ohio General Assembly fund the cost of the 120 legal aid attorneys and support staff who were laid off because of declining funds.

Three years later, we're still waiting for the General Assembly to respond.

**These kinds of disparities demean
the criminal justice system**
March 30, 2019, The Columbus Dispatch

Jeffrey Epstein, a Miami hedge fund manager, and
Kevin Keith, an indigent Bucyrus resident, have been
through the criminal justice system for serious crimes
but with remarkably different experiences.

Epstein allegedly had sex with and trafficked over three
dozen girls, most of them 13 to 16. He faced a life
sentence in 2007, but his lawyers worked a deal. Epstein
served just 13 months in a county jail and was allowed
work at his Palm Beach office during the day.

Keith was sent to Death Row in 1994 for three murders
and three attempted murders. Post-trial investigations
revealed that a state crime lab analyst contrived forensic
evidence to link Keith to the shootings and that the state
suppressed evidence.

Epstein is a multimillionaire, white, and could afford
high profile lawyers Alan Dershowitz and Kenneth Starr.
Keith is black and couldn't afford to hire his own
lawyer.

Shocking? Yes. Surprising? No.

Disparities in the criminal justice system begin with
where you are born. The Brookings Institution reports
that boys raised in families in the bottom 10 percent of
income are 20 times more likely to be incarcerated in

their early 30s than boys born to the wealthiest families. Boys born in the lowest income families make up roughly 27 percent of 30-year old inmates.

According to the advocacy group Sentencing Project, racial disparities exist because of policies and practices, implicit bias and stereotypes in decision making, and structural disadvantages. Bryan Stephenson's "Just Mercy" provides several troubling examples.

Nearly 1.5 million people were incarcerated in federal and state prisons in 2016. Of these 440,200 were white, 487,300 were black and 339,600 were Hispanic, though blacks and Hispanics make up just 13 and 18 percent of the nation's population, respectively. Research shows that the race of the victim and defendant influences sentencing. Killing a white person increases the likelihood of a death sentence, and blacks are more likely than whites to be sentenced to death.

New York City's "stop and frisk" policy illustrates the problems cited by the Sentencing Project. Police were permitted to stop anyone for "furtive" behavior"— whatever that is. A federal court found in 2013 the police stopped 4.4 million people over eight years. Fifty-two percent were black, and 10 percent were white, but blacks made up just 23 percent of the population, while whites comprised 33 percent.

Which group was more often found to have weapons and other contraband? Whites, by a tiny margin.

Let's tie all this into Keith's case. Police were told a "large black man" was seen where the shootings occurred, and Keith is six feet tall, black, weighs 300 pounds and had been previously arrested for selling a small amount of crack. His arrest may have made sense, but nothing that followed did.

Keith was watching TV and surprised when the police arrested him—not what you would expect of someone who shot six people just two days prior. Forensics from the scene—carpet fibers, fingerprints—didn't connect Keith to the shooting. A seven-year-old survivor of the shooting said the shooter was her daddy's friend, Bruce; based on a photo, she ruled out Keith, who had multiple alibi witnesses.

But the police had their man. From then on, a case was constructed against Keith. Bogus forensic links to the scene were created, and favorable evidence was suppressed. Fortunately, Keith's sentence was commuted in 2010 to life, and a federal appellate court recently granted him the opportunity to persuade a federal district court that he should receive a new trial.

One of Keith's attorneys, Rachal G. Troutman, puts it this way: "It takes a tremendous amount of time, energy, and resources to undo a wrongful conviction, most of which could be avoided by providing more resources to poor defendants from the beginning."

Do all indigent blacks get abused like Keith? No. Do all wealthy white men get sweetheart deals like Epstein did?

No. But can you imagine someone like Keith getting treated the way Epstein did?

The Slow Death of
the English Language

Stop the bad grammar!
*Winter 2013, Columbus Bar Association Lawyers
Quarterly*

In the words of a great American nautical hero, "I've had
all I can stands. I can't stands it no more!" I'm talking
about bad grammar. That's right—bad grammar, a bad
practice that is becoming commonplace. I hear TV
journalists using bad grammar. I see grammatical errors
in newspapers and books. Worse yet, I hear bad
grammar from lawyers.

Language is the most important tool we employ. It is the
palette from which we convey ideas and the means by
which we persuade and influence. Language is what our
profession is all about, and we should all be masters in
its use.

So, where does one turn for help with grammar
questions? Simple—there are plenty of resources
available, and I reviewed three before writing this
piece.[41] I also enjoy an advantage provided by my
parents. I was rigorously schooled on the subject of
grammar by Dominican nuns (aka the penguins) during
my formative years.

So, let's begin with some of the more common examples
of bad grammar. The first is, "Him and I played on the
same softball team." What? I hear this somewhat

---

[41] "Sleeping Dogs Don't Lay" by Richard Lederer and Richard
Dowis; "Woe is I" by Patricia T. O'Conner; "Good Grief, Good
Grammar" by Dianna Booher.

routinely. Would you say, "Him played on the same softball team"?[42] Of course not. "Him" has to follow a preposition (for those of you not trained by the penguins, prepositions are words such as "to" or "with") and cannot be the subject of a sentence. Proper grammar demands that one say, "He and I played on the same softball team."

Here's an error I'm starting to hear all too frequently: "Return the book to Joe or I." Oh, how the grammar gods frown when they hear this. Would you say, "Return the book to I"? Of course not. You would say, "Return the book to me," which means you should say, "Return the book to Joe or me."

An error related to the one above is, "It is Debbie and I's anniversary." Agggghhh! Please stop the madness! Would you say, "It is I's anniversary"? Of course not. You would say, "It is my anniversary." There are eyes, and there are ayes, but there is no I's. There never was, and there never will be. Who started this trend? In the world of grammar, this type of language abuse is akin to a capital crime.

Here's one I am starting to see in the newspapers: "The couple have two children." Wait a minute—a couple is but one unit, and so the word "has" should be used, as in, "The couple has two children." Don't be led astray by the fact that a couple is composed of two people. As we say in court, that's irrelevant.

---

[42]   Yes, I know. The placement of the question mark in this sentence raises punctuation questions. That's an issue for another day.

A close cousin of this error concerns the word data. I'm starting to see with some regularity the phrase, "The data are inconclusive." I suppose some modern linguist concluded that, because it refers to multiple bits of information, the word data is plural. Really? So, by analogy would you say, "The army are advancing"? Of course not. Sure, an army is composed of many soldiers, but an army itself comprises a single unit. Besides, "the army are advancing" sounds dumb—almost as dumb as "the data are inconclusive." "The data is inconclusive" is the way to go.[43]

Here's another common mistake: "If anyone calls, tell them I'm out and schedule them for a meeting." Why use the word "them" when we're talking about "anyone," which refers to single person. The correct statement is, "If anyone calls, tell him I'm out and schedule him for a meeting." Ah, but that's politically incorrect, some would say. To avoid any gender preference, the PC police mandate that we say, "If anyone calls, tell him or her I'm out and schedule him or her for a meeting." Really? This stuff makes my head explode.[44]

Is submission to political correctness so necessary that we are forced to use stilted language? Oh, puhhhhlease. Do people really get offended over this stuff? Doesn't, "If anyone calls, tell him I'm out and schedule him for

---

[43] Since writing this piece, I've taken some heat for what I had to say about data. Too bad. This is my position, and I'm sticking to it.
[44] I've taken heat for this one, as well. My response? Same as above.

an appointment" sound better? Here's my view: if anybody has a problem with what I'm saying, he can give me a call.

For those of you who feel constrained to oblige the dictates of the PC police but still strive for some modicum of eloquence, here's another option. Try to avoid using a pronoun. "If anyone calls, please say that I'm out and schedule the caller for an appointment." There you go—problem avoided.

Thank you for letting me vent. I feel better now. In the next edition of *Lawyers Quarterly*, look for the sequel, "Is there a moral imperative to correcting someone's bad grammar in public?"

I'm done with you guys
Summer 2014, Columbus Bar Association Lawyer's Quarterly Magazine

It's almost too much to bear. It's enough to make my head explode. Our English language is slowly degrading to a point where things that were once considered to be bad grammar and offensive slang are now slowly becoming the new standards.

Using the correct pronoun after a conjunction is a lost art. No one these days gets the following phrase correct: "Contact either Joe or me." Instead, you will always hear, "Contact either Joe or I." Perhaps the problem is that we no longer have nuns whacking grade school students on the backs of their hands for these grammatical sins, but then Catholics are not the only ones who are failing; bad grammar knows no religious boundaries. Still, I wonder why the problem seems to be getting worse.

Could it be that I'm just getting older and, therefore, grumpier, or (as I prefer to think) are people just getting increasingly lazy about the rules? Maybe I'm just old fashioned. I wear suspenders and pleated pants, and I don't wear my ball cap backwards.

In any case, the latest source of frustration for me is the phrase, "you guys." Oh, my, how I have grown to hate this phrase. For reasons unknown, it has come to replace the second person, plural form of "you." It is almost a given that when addressing a group, a person will ask,

"What are *you guys* doing?" Apparently, to ask, "What are you doing" would leave some doubt regarding who is being addressed.

I heard Savannah Guthrie on *The Today Show* ask a mother and her daughters, "What did this mean for you guys?" (I was watching morning TV because I was on vacation.) So, a mid-30's mom and her two middle school-age daughters are "guys?" Something is wrong here. I suspect Walter Cronkite is rolling in his grave.

I've heard young adult women address each other as "you guys." I don't get it. I've heard attorneys use the same slang when addressing a jury. "Now, when you go into the jury room, I want you guys to think about . . ." Really? What's next? Maybe, " 'Sup, Judge?"

But wait, there's more. People have tried to use "you guys" as a plural, possessive adjective. Instead of hearing, "I like your house," you will often hear, "I like you guys' house" or perhaps "your guys' house" and—my favorite—"your guyses' house." The only good thing about such bad grammar is that it provides a moment of amusement. Because none of these phrases rolls off the tongue, you can sense a speaker's discomfort in trying to articulate a phrase that, down deep, he knows isn't quite right yet feels compelled to say anyway. It's sort of a verbal stumbling.

When my wife and I were dining at a restaurant some weeks back, our waiter, a nice young man, ended practically every phrase with "you guys." "How are you

guys this evening? . . . Can I get a drink for you guys? . .
. How does everything taste, you guys?" The server
who brought the appetizer asked, "One of you guys had
the meatball?" I admit my wife has to muster a certain
amount of fortitude and stamina to put up with me, but I
don't think that merits her being called a "guy." Need I
speak of the age difference between the waiter and either
my wife or me?

A friend of mine commented that the use of "you guys"
is emblematic of an overall change in our language that
requires adjustment from grumps like me. Oh, please.
Sure, language changes over time. We no longer say
things like, "That's jolly good, old boy," which,
according to Doris Kearns Goodwin in *The Bully Pulpit*,
was how people spoke in the days of Teddy Roosevelt.

"You guys" is in another category. It is slang that goes
too far and denigrates our language, and language—the
thing that connects and defines us—is too important.
When we allow our language to degrade, we lose
something important.

I'll admit there's a place in the world for "you guys" or
some derivative. If you live in New Jersey, you can refer
to your friends as "yous guys." If you live in Chicago, it
makes sense to refer to the people in the next
neighborhood as "dem guys." If you're a cop in New
York City, everyone would understand if you referred to
the local Mafioso as "wise guys." If you're *a guy*
greeting the *other guys* in your golf league, it's
acceptable to say, "How are you guys doing this

afternoon?" There are other acceptable uses, but generally they should be limited in frequency and, for the most part, to exchanges between males who are contemporaries.

Political and Social Issues

Ohio biz not immune from human trafficking
February 22, 2013, Columbus Business First

It is a fact of life only recently coming to light. Human beings are being trafficked in Ohio, either for sex or forced labor.

Victims, generally foreign nationals and women, are forced to work 10 to 16 hours a day, seven days a week. Trafficking perpetuates because of the demand for low cost, unskilled labor for kitchen work, cleaning, agriculture and factory production and goes undetected because work places are not monitored.

The Polaris Project, an outreach organization, explains that trafficking begins with promises of steady employment and wages—hope for someone with no hope. As one woman recounted, "I was an easy target for my trafficker. I was a desperate mother looking for a way to provide for my three children. I was told that I would have a good job with good pay and a place where to live."

The promises never materialize.

"When I got here," continued the woman, "I was locked in the factory and forced to work 17 to 18 hours a day, seven days a week."

Control is maintained by preying on fear. Immigration papers are confiscated, and victims are threatened with deportation. Victims often have little command of English, are unfamiliar with laws and are scared. Based on their experience with corrupt authorities in their countries, they are afraid to go to the police. Add some physical and sexual abuse, and control becomes absolute.

Rand Corporation conducted a study of trafficking in Toledo and Columbus in 2007. Both cities were considered prime locations because of proximity to highway systems, growing immigrant populations, agriculture, and large universities and corporations. Five cases were discovered in Columbus. One involved Russian immigrants on tourist visas who were forced to clean hotels against their will. In three cases, immigrants from Ethiopia, Eritrea and Guinea were brought here on promises of domestic work; upon arriving, they were confined and forced to work long hours without pay. In the fifth case, a businessman from Morocco enslaved his wife and forced her to work.

The Polaris Project reported about a young Philippino woman who was recruited and brought to the U.S. by two Milwaukee doctors in 1985. Until rescued 19 years later, she was forced to work, forbidden to go outside and threatened with arrest and deportation. The ABC news show *Nightline* reported in June 2008 about two Indonesian women who had been held captive in a Long Island mansion, where they were forced to work and regularly beaten since 2002.

 The U.S. Department of State estimated in 2010 that 12.3 million people are trafficked worldwide. Most victims come from Thailand, Mexico, the Philippines,

Haiti, India, Guatemala and the Dominican Republic. The Department of Justice has estimated that 14,500 to 17,500 are trafficked in the U.S. While more investigations focus on sex trafficking, labor trafficking involves more victims.

In 2000, the government enacted the Trafficking Victims Protection Act, which focuses on victims who are subjected to "force, fraud, or coercion for the purpose of subjection to involuntary servitude." The act provided education about trafficking, collaboration with other countries, hot lines and other sources of support for victims but was allowed to expire in 2011.

Ohio took action in 2011. It is now a first degree felony in Ohio to take action that results in another person being subjected to involuntary servitude or compelled to engage in sex for hire. To show that a victim was "compelled," the state need only prove that her will was overcome by force, fear, duress or intimidation. A conviction carries a jail sentence of 10 to 15 years. It is a third degree felony to destroy or confiscate a government ID or passport for the purpose of facilitating trafficking, punishable by nine to 36 months of jail time.

Ohio enacted additional legislation in June 2012. The attorney general is now required to publish annual statistical data concerning trafficking. Police officers now receive training in investigating and handling human trafficking.

Take a closer look at the people around you. Does the person washing dishes at a restaurant or doing nails at a salon have a distant stare, or are her eyes cast down, and does she look scared and alone?

If you suspect trafficking is taking place or would like training on the issue or help for a victim, contact the National Human Trafficking Resource Center at NHTRC@polarisproject.org or 888-3737-888.

Time for a tough talk on fracking's inevitable danger
March 7, 2014, Columbus Business First

Some weeks back, the news carried reports about a newly discovered by-product of hydraulic fracturing—radioactive waste. While the oil and gas industry vigorously promote the safety of fracking, as it is commonly known, we need to be concerned about several things.

First, the industry has done its best to downplay the dangers. When speaking before the Downtown Kiwanis Club two years ago, Tom Stewart, executive director of the Ohio Oil and Gas Association, stated that all chemicals used in the process would be disclosed. As it turns out, the statute dealing with disclosure contains an exception for chemicals that fracking companies classify as trade secrets.

Second, the promise of jobs has suppressed environmental concerns. When promoting legislation, you can move mountains by using one of two magic phrases: "this will create jobs" or "this will be good for small business." Whether you can prove either doesn't seem to matter. But say either phrase enough, and it creates such momentum that environment issues are given scant attention.

Third, the industry is aided by too close of a relationship with government, both at the regulatory and legislative level. In 2012, representatives of the Ohio Department of Natural Resources, the agency mandated to regulate fracking, spoke at a legal education program about the fracking. They acted more like advocates than regulators—much talk about the benefits but no discussion about the potential hazards.

The *Dispatch* revealed that the ODNR had drafted a 10-page memo about fracking that was critical of environmentalists and warned that "legal countermeasures and crisis readiness" by the state would be necessary in dealing with them. The memo also stated the need to enlist industry help to minimize the public's concerns.

Apparently aware of its own wrongheaded allegiance, ODNR recognized that its public relations efforts "could blur public perception of ODNR's regulatory role in oil and gas" which would require "precise messaging and coordination" to counteract. While the memo may not have been implemented, its message is still troubling.

We see the tie between the industry and the legislature in the current debate over how much of a severance tax should be levied on gas. The *Cincinnati Enquirer* reported last July that the ten largest oil and gas companies contributed over $600,000 to Ohio legislators since 2010; 91 percent of the money went to Republicans, and $227,000 went to House Speaker William G. Batchelder, R-Medina, alone. Who's opposing Gov. John Kasich on the severance tax he proposes? Batchelder and other Republicans.

The situation is reminiscent of President Teddy Roosevelt's fight to end the collusion that existed between the railroads and oil companies. Republican Senate leadership opposed Roosevelt's efforts and, as described by Doris Kearns Goodwin in "The Bully Pulpit," was seen as "representative of the trusts" that controlled trade and was "in thrall to the business interests that filled their coffers through campaign contributions."

Wherever there is human endeavor, there will be error. The oil and gas industry tells us it will always operate safely, and so we need not be alarmed. Really? Show me an industry involved in high risk operations, and I'll show you a catastrophe. Think off-shore drilling leaks, underground mine explosions, airplane crashes, train derailments and so on. Things will go badly wrong with fracking—an explosion, a fireball, a chemical spill. It's a matter of time. Will we be ready to respond?

I understand that fracking is here to stay, and I'm glad we have this resource to exploit, but the availability of a resource doesn't end the discussion. The questions are, what net benefit will fracking provide, and how we will we handle the consequences of fracking? Fracking is expensive in ways that get little attention: the wear and tear on roads that were not designed to handle large volumes of heavy trucks; the depletion of water sources needed in the drilling process; the transportation and handling of wastewater from drilling; and the disasters that are almost certain to happen.

These are the issues that require our attention. Now that fracking is here to stay, can we start having meaningful conversations about them?

Lawmakers "fighting" for us hardly helping
July 11, 2014, Columbus Business First

Have you noticed all the fighting that goes on at the statehouse and in the Capitol? It's hardly a secret—lawmakers regularly tell us they are fighting for us. Think about how often you hear the phrase.

Are our legislators really fighting, or do they actually mean they are advocating a position? Should we care about the language they use? Am I just being too particular about what some might characterize as a figure of speech?

Maybe not. Let's put this in context and look at the big picture. When's the last time you saw Democrats and Republicans playing nice together and moving forward in a cooperative way? Do you remember anything except acrimony from either political party? Have you seen the two sides working constructively? No. All the statesmen who knew how to negotiate and work a deal have left and gone home. Legislators like former senator George V. Voinovich are becoming a thing of the past.

Considering that both state and federal lawmakers routinely engage in a process that is more akin to fighting, I think words do matter, and I think our lawmakers are telling us exactly what they're doing. Think about it. Words define our intentions. They describe how we feel, and how we intend to act. So, when a lawmaker says that he's fighting for something, he establishes a mindset where listening, reasoning and discussion are not on his agenda. He's set to fight, which means a lot of talking and no listening and being critical of anyone with a different view. The goal is to win. Period!

What's really remarkable about this fighting attitude is that it sometimes seems that only our legislators have it. Think about how you handle differences of opinion and different goals in your personal life. Do you "fight" with your wife that you should be able to play golf every Saturday, or do you try to persuade her? At worst, maybe you gently argue about the benefits of golfing with your buds, but if you're fighting with your wife, you'll soon have bigger problems than a few missed golf outings.

What about when you disagree with your boss? Rather than hostile discourse, you probably try to nudge him into seeing your position and show him that you can improve whatever you're both concerned about. You don't fight with him, do you? You want to keep your job, right?

Same thing when it comes to your business partners. Fight with your business partner long enough, and soon the business begins to suffer. Fight too much, and your partner hires an attorney and asks the court to appoint a receiver.

In any healthy relationship—personal or business—we wouldn't think about referring to how we interact with others as fighting. We say we have disagreements or that we don't see eye-to-eye, but fighting? No, we know deep down that to suggest that we're fighting with people who are close to us means we're at a dead end in the relationship—and in big trouble.

So, why do we do it in the political context? Maybe legislators have lost sight of the big picture. Like it or not, we're in this together, and we can succeed only to the extent that we cooperate. That means trying to persuade while also listening.

When we go enter highly charged situations with the idea that we're fighting for something, there can't be any dialogue because, by definition, we're fighting, and you only fight with enemies. You can't engage an enemy in meaningful conversation. The result is a group of talking heads, each repeating his position, while being deaf to the other side—a death spiral of sorts.

So, yes, words matter. I suspect that even the most uncompromising legislators who think they have to fight for their constituents live their lives differently when it comes to their spouses and staffs. To do otherwise would mean they suffer miserably at home and in their offices. Then again, maybe some legislators were born to fight— and enjoy it.

Rwanda could teach U.S. about collaboration
May 7, 2017, The Columbus Dispatch

What a can the United States learn from Rwanda? It would seem, little. The U.S. is a large, industrialized nation, with nearly 325,000,000 people, a gross domestic product of $18 trillion, and an average life expectancy of 78 years. Rwanda is a tiny, developing country of only 11 million people, with a poor infrastructure and insufficient access to electricity, and an average life expectancy of 64.5 years.

More about what we can learn from Rwanda in a minute. First, let's review Rwanda's 1994 civil war, when the Hutu majority tried to exterminate the Tutsi minority. In just 100 days, nearly one million people were slaughtered. The weapon of choice was the machete.

Rwanda has since purposefully endeavored to promote unity and forgiveness. The process is called Umuganda, where everyone—including those who took part in the slaughter and those who survived it—work side by side on community projects. Participation is mandatory. "Umuganda is about the culture of working together and helping each other to build this country," said Paul Kagame, president of Rwanda.

Rwanda has also implemented a restorative justice program, where those who participated in the genocide can be released from jail if they seek forgiveness from the survivors whose family members were killed. There are villages where former killers and survivors eat and work together, a process that required years of effort.

What's the connection to the U.S.? We may not be hacking each other with machetes, but we suffer from a divisiveness that is harmful in other ways. We're at the point where we cannot even tolerate different points of view. The University California at Berkeley cancelled a guest appearance on April 27 by conservative writer, Ann Coulter, for fear her appearance would lead to violence.

The Coulter controversy followed violent clashes between supporters of President Donald Trump and his left-wing critics at a pro-Trump rally in the city of Berkeley. Apparently, the ballot box does not end disputes. Fighting in the streets over politically ideology is becoming acceptable.

Then again, the political machine we have accepted has set the tone. Congressional districts are purposefully drawn to favor the majority party. National unity and giving a voice to everyone were not the goal in creating these districts. Subjugating the minority was.

A Dispatch editorial illustrated how Ohio's congressional districts split county boundaries 54 times, and seven counties are split among three or more districts. The ninth district, a thin strip of land that crosses the northern portion of five counties bordering the lake, is known as the "snake by the lake." Whatever was necessary to maintain the majority in power was the order of the day when the districts were created.

Members of opposing political parties don't talk with other. Instead, they talk at each other with carefully crafted sound bites. While legislators might speak with courtesy on the House or Senate floor, it's a different story outside where they forget about the issues and pillory their opponents.

Regrettably, President Trump has contributed to the problem. Rather than attend the White House Correspondents' Association Dinner on April 29, he spoke at a political rally in Harrsiburg, Pa., where he told the crowd, "I could not possibly be more thrilled than to be … spending my evening with all of you and with a much, much larger crowd and much better people, right?" Since when did the people in Harrisburg become better people than those in Washington, D.C., and why is the president unabashed about criticizing the people in his own neighborhood?

The hate that exists is palpable. People are beaten at rallies, and banners display hate speech. But divisive talk does only one thing: it spawns more division and more anger. Nothing good comes of it. Ever.

The only way to change things is to break the cycle. Instead of talking at an opponent, you have to learn to listen to your opponent. Stephen Covey, author of "The 7 Habits of Highly Effective People," instructs us to "seek first to understand, then to be understood."

A marvelous thing happens when you apply Covey's paradigm: you see your opponent in a new light. You appreciate his point of view and see him as a human being who has worth, not some miserable cur who you feel justified denigrating.

Respect starts to enter the relationship, and suddenly things change. Now, you and your opponent can move to common ground and perhaps find a solution. Division gives way to collaboration. Progress follows.

It's a lesson the people in Rwanda were able to learn, as evidenced by the country's growth in GDP from $1.3 billion in 1995 to nearly $8 billion today. Perhaps the difference is that 64 percent of the seats in the last parliamentary elections were filled by women.

Trump pushes agenda with criticism of judge
December 8, 2017, Columbus Dispatch

Two years ago, Kathryn Steinle was killed by Jose Garcia Zarate, an illegal immigrant who had been deported five times and had a history of drug convictions. On Nov. 30, Zarate was acquitted in Steinle's murder trial. President Donald Trump called it "a disgraceful verdict."

It's a shocking and a horrible result for Steinle's family, because there's no doubt Zarate was the shooter. Was Trump right to criticize the verdict and, by implication, the jury?

Trump also took issue with the trial judge for not allowing in evidence about Zarate's background: "The jury was not told the killer of Kate was a 7 time felon. The Schumer/Pelosi Democrats are so weak on Crime that they will pay a big price in the 2018 and 2020 Elections." Was Trump right to criticize the judge?

First, let's look at the entire picture. Steinle was walking with her father along a pier in San Francisco when she was struck by a bullet. According to the L.A. Times, Zarate fired a single shot. The bullet hit the concrete just 12 feet ahead of him, ricocheted and then traveled 78 feet before hitting Steinle. When interviewed by police, Zarate said he had found the gun, which had been stolen, wrapped in a rag and that it accidentally fired when he picked it up.

Zarate was tried for first degree murder, which is killing
with premeditation or in conjunction with another crime,
such as rape, and second degree murder, which is killing
impulsively but without premeditation. He was also tried
for involuntary manslaughter. The judge did not allow
the prosecution to present evidence about Zarate's
immigration status, deportations or drug convictions.
The jury was allowed to consider only whether Zarate
intentionally, recklessly or negligently shot Steinle.

According to Fox News, the jury deliberated for 30
hours before acquitting Zarate on all three counts. He
was found guilty only of unlawful possession of a
firearm.

Let's look at Trump's comments in reverse order. Was
the judge wrong for not allowing in evidence about
Zarate's past? No. The rules of evidence, which vary to
some degree for each state, generally do not permit
evidence of a defendant's past bad acts to be admitted at
trial so that the jury is not prejudiced against him. We
want a defendant's guilt to be based solely on the facts
presented at trial, not on his past.

This isn't a matter of being weak on crime, as Trump
contends. This is a matter of a long-standing rule of
evidence that serves everyone who is tried. This same
evidentiary rule also applies to civil law cases. If Trump
ever goes to trial, he too will benefit from this rule.

Was Trump right to criticize the jury? As long as human
beings are involved in any endeavor, there will always

be error, but let's look closely at the process. I like the
analysis of Mark O'Mara, the attorney who defended
George Zimmerman in the Trayvon Martin case.

O'Mara was interviewed on Dec. 2 by CNN journalist
Michael Smerconish and thinks the verdict was proper.
That doesn't mean he likes the verdict, because he
doesn't. Who could? But the jury did its job to the best
of its ability. If fault is to be found, Mara finds fault with
the district attorney's office for overplaying its hand and
charging Zarate with first degree murder when the facts
weren't there.

Jurors decide cases based on the written instructions they
receive. Those instructions are agreed upon by the
attorneys for both sides, and if they can't agree, the final
decision rests with the judge. Maybe a more narrow
focus on the key facts and trying Zarate on fewer counts
would have yielded a different result.

O'Mara takes issue with politicians who criticize the
criminal justice system for political purposes and said
Trump was wrong to call the verdict disgraceful. O'Mara
also showed his displeasure with former president
Barack Obama for having "chimed in twice" during the
Zimmerman case. "It's horribly improper and degrades
the system for any politician … to come in and attack the
system."

If you haven't sat through the entire trial and listened to
all the testimony and viewed all the evidence, as jurors
do, you've got no business second-guessing their verdict.

Deciding a case is tough work. Talk to experienced trial lawyers, and you'll hear them say that jurors work hard to arrive at the best decision.

Trump's anger has more to do with his agenda on immigration reform and building a wall, but those are subjects separate and apart. Admittedly, Trump is right the immigration system failed by allowing Zarate to be here in the first place, but let's not give Trump credit for recognizing what's obvious.

Is choosing death with dignity a moral decision?
August 8, 2018, The Columbus Dispatch

After being terminally ill for months or perhaps years, should you have the right to say, "I've had enough. It's time to die?" Not only a tough question, it's one that makes us uneasy.

Seven states—California, Colorado, Hawaii, Montana, Oregon, Vermont, Washington—and the District of Columbia permit what some call "death with dignity." Except for Montana, the laws are similar: patients must be a resident of the state, capable of making and communicating health care decisions for themselves, at least 18 years old, and diagnosed with a terminal illness that will lead to death within six months. Patients must also make two oral requests, at least 15 days apart, and one written request.

Polar views are voiced by Peter Singer, philosopher and professor of bioethics at Princeton University, and Dr. Ilora Finlay, former president of the British Medical Association.

Singer believes, "There are circumstances in which the person who is considering death wants to die. That is their autonomous choice. So, death is not a violation of their autonomy, or contrary to their strongest wishes … there are cases in which a person has no more valuable life to look forward to—valuable by their judgment, not valuable by somebody's else's judgment."

Finlay sees too much risk. "When you normalize physician-assisted suicide., the underlying social dynamic changes. Laws send a message. And the message they send is that if you're terminally ill, ending your life is something that you probably ought to think about."

Why is it we have concluded that months, and sometimes years, of chronic pain are not grounds to end one's life? The common response: only God has that right, yet we make exceptions to that rule. No one questions the right to take a life to defend his own or another's. Capital punishment exists in 31 states. Even among those who oppose abortion, many believe abortion is morally acceptable when a mother's life is at risk.

But taking one's life to escape a prolonged and painful illness is another matter.

Sen. Charleta B. Tavares, D-Columbus, shares Singer's perspective. In April, she introduced S.B. 249, which is modeled after Oregon's law. Tavares acted in response to concerns expressed by constituents who are members of Death with Dignity, a non-profit that believes qualified terminally ill people should have the right to make their own end-of-life decisions.

Tavares sees a big distinction between suicide and S.B. 249, and she doesn't like the bill being coined as "physician-assisted suicide." She explains that when people commit suicide, "they are generally suffering from a disorder, are not terminally ill, and they make the decision to end their life spontaneously. They die alone and in the state of despair."

Tavares lost a brother to suicide and is a strong advocate for suicide prevention programs. She doesn't see any inconsistency with S.B. 249. People who will benefit from S.B. 249 "already know they are about to die," says Tavares. "They simply want the chance to stop their suffering and their family's suffering. They want to control how they will depart. They are making a rational decision."

A study by the Journal of the American Medical Association evidences that Oregon's law is used somewhat minimally. During an 18-year period, 1545 prescriptions for lethal medications were written, and 991 patients died by using those prescriptions, meaning patients changed their minds. The median age for patients was 71. The large majority suffered from cancer.

Tavares and those who believe in death with dignity aren't asking others to change their moral beliefs. They just want to provide an end-of-life option to those who want it. Shouldn't they be able to say, "I've suffered long and hard. I've had enough. So has my family. I'd like the peace that death brings."

Confronting death is scary. Perhaps morality gives us a veil to hide behind.

More diversity would make for a better Congress
November 4, 2018, The Columbus Dispatch

If you haven't noticed, Congress doesn't represent a cross-section of America. Its members comprise a narrow sector of the nation, and that's a problem for reasons I'll discuss in a minute. First, let's look at the numbers.

Non-Hispanic whites make up 61 percent of our population, but 80 percent of representatives and senators are white. People 60 years old or older make up just 20 percent of the population but the average age of a representative is 57; for a senator it's 61. The average age of Republican committee chairs in the House is 59. Ranking House Democrats average 68. Eighteen of the 33 senators up for re-election this fall are over 65 years old.

The Senate Judiciary Committee, the committee that vets judicial candidates, is comprised of 16 white males, whose average age is 64. Only four females and one black male are on the committee.

Should we be concerned? Only if better decision-making matters to you. Studies show that diversity tends to improve workplace performance. Though people generally prefer to spend time with others who are similar to them, a homogenous workplace does not always produce the best results.

Katherine Phillips, professor at the Northwestern University Kellogg School of Management, explains that diversity "often comes with more cognitive processing and more exchange of information and more perceptions of conflict." Phillips touts diversity because it allows new ideas to emerge and people to learn from one another.

A simple experiment Phillips conducted in 2010 with professors from Brigham Young University and Stanford University illustrates the point. Phillips assembled 50 same-gender three-person groups comprised of fraternity and sorority members. Before being assigned to a group, each participant was asked to read a series of interviews conducted by a detective investigating a murder and tasked with deciding the most likely suspect.

A 20-minute time limit was set for reaching a conclusion, but five minutes into the process, a newcomer, either from the same fraternity or sorority or from a different fraternity or sorority, joined the group and engaged in the deliberation.

Not surprising, the original three-person groups felt more comfortable with a newcomer who belonged to their same fraternity or sorority, but the groups with newcomers from a different fraternity or sorority arrived at the correct answer far more frequently than the homogenous groups Even more interesting is that, while the homogenous groups did not perform as well, they were more confident about their decisions than the better performing diverse groups.

An eight-year study of a large global company by Sara F. Ellison of MIT and Wallace P. Mullin of George Washington University, published in 2014, produced similar results. Employees were found to be more cooperative in homogenous units but seemed to be less productive. While gender diversity, on the other hand, can have a detrimental effect on cooperation and trust, this consequence is outweighed by the improved office performance, including revenue gain, that comes with diversity.

McKinsey & Co., a global management consulting firm, examined financial data from 2010 to 2013 for 366 companies in the U.S, the United Kingdom, Canada and Latin America. The findings? Greater gender and ethnic diversity translate into more profit.

Why is this? Companies committed to diversity have access to a larger talent pool, and a commitment to diversity more closely aligns companies to the more diverse customer bases they serve. Diversity fosters positive attitudes and behaviors in the workplace, and a diverse team of thinkers is inclined to challenge one another and be more willing to explore new ideas.

There are myriad reasons why Congress is dysfunctional. The system is captive to party politics, lobbyists and money, and gerrymandering guarantees reelection for many members. The limited pool from which Congress draws its ranks adds to the problem.

There's nothing wrong with old white men. I'm one myself. But when it's largely old white men calling the shots, the chances decrease for new perspectives, ideas and change.

Establishing and maintaining a culture of accountability is crucial

August 2, 2019, The Columbus Dispatch

We want them to protect us and maintain law and order. We authorize them to use force, lethal, if necessary, and we expect them to get it right every time. And when the police err, we get angry.

We've seen a number of police shootings nationwide, and the shootings that cause us concern often involve white officers shooting black men. The optics aren't good, as they say, and the question that always follows is, were the officer's actions justified? But there's a more important question: how do we minimize mistakes?

Because it's hard to make sense of what we see, I spent some time with Commander Robert Meader, who leads the Columbus Division of Police Training Bureau, and three of his instructors. Before getting to that, let's look at the big picture.

In 2017, Columbus police responded to over 600,000 incidents, resulting in 22,228 custodial arrests. Force—everything from throwing a punch to using a firearm—was used 438 times; firearms were used 13 times. That same year, the police recovered 2750 firearms—that's seven guns a day—the large majority of which were not lawfully possessed.

Meader invited me to participate in live training that involves realistic scenarios. It was eye-opening. I didn't recognize potential threats until it was too late. My performance was, well, not good.

I watched recruits perform. Besides dealing with potential and obvious threats, there's the stress element and dealing with distractions. You hope the training takes over instinctively and the recruits will think clearly and not emotionally, but mistakes are made. And when a recruit errs, instructors move in to discuss what went wrong and alternatives that were overlooked.

Back to the primary question: how do we minimize mistakes? Let's start with the premise they're inevitable. As Meader puts it, "We only hire imperfect human beings because that's all that's available." He places emphasis on the culture of a police department and advocates a culture of training, accountability and discipline.

"We train beyond the standards mandated for us," Meader says. Minimizing errors is a matter of good initial training, realistic scenarios and continuing education, his instructors explained. Meader stated it's a matter of "trying to develop good habit patterns, similar to muscle memory in sports. And what we do has to comply with the law, and so we regularly train on legal issues that affect our work."

When there's a problem, the situation is investigated, and, if warranted, remedial training is mandated. The mistakes made by officers are used as training opportunities for others. It's how you develop, Meader says, "a culture of accountability."

Still, there are complications. The Plain View project revealed that several Philadelphia police officers were posting bigoted and hate-filled posts on social media. Were warning signs overlooked? Can these officers be trusted? Should they be required to undergo evaluation, or should they be dismissed? The point is, there are subsurface issues that affect the integrity of a police force and have to be dealt with.

And there's the matter of what the public thinks it knows about police work from the usually unrealistic world of TV and movies. Our predetermined attitudes set our expectations when we watch body cam footage.

Adding to the complexity is the judicial system. Sometimes police officers are not indicted or are acquitted in situations that to the public call for a different result. Juries—there's that human element again—can get things wrong. Or maybe these are situations where we think we know better, even though we didn't sit through the grand jury proceedings or trial and listen to all the testimony and see all the evidence.

At the risk of appearing to be an apologist for law enforcement, where there is human endeavor, there will always be error. The best we can do is conduct routine training and remedial training, when required, and foster

a culture of accountability and discipline so as to
minimize mistakes.

LGTBQ rights pose no threat to religious freedom
November 26, 2019, The Columbus Dispatch

Are religious freedoms under attack? Gays have the right to marry. The U.S. Supreme Court has left open the question whether a baker must decorate a wedding cake and a florist must provide floral arrangements to be used at gay weddings, and the court is now deciding whether employers can discriminate against LGBTQ employees.

Can society mandate equal treatment for LGBTQ people while respecting the beliefs of those who say their religion precludes them doing anything that condones what they see as sinful?

Let's look at our social contract. We established as a fundamental truth nearly 250 years ago that we are all created equal, with the unalienable rights of life, liberty and the pursuit of happiness. To make this work, we agreed to live under a set of rules, and those rules have evolved over time. Slavery was once permissible, women couldn't vote, and interracial marriage was illegal.

Certain religious groups demand they should be free to deny goods and services, even employment, to gays, not because of their sexual identity—that would be judgmental and wrong, they say. It's that they don't want to do anything that might be construed as condoning sexual mores they find to be objectionable.

So it is, that a baker objects to decorating a cake, and a florist objects to creating flower arrangements for a gay wedding. Similarly, the owner of a funeral home believes he would be endorsing a transgender employee's denial of his gender at birth—and disobeying God's law—by continuing to employ the employee during his sex transition.

But would that same florist and baker object to selling their goods to an adulterer who is purchasing gifts for his mistress? Likely not, for how would they know of the customer's adultery. But what if the adultery were exposed, what then? By selling to the adulterer, wouldn't the baker and florist be condoning the customer's extramarital affair?

If homosexuality and adultery are a sin, then the baker and florist should inquire of all their customers as to how those cakes and flowers will be used. And perhaps employers should ask job applicants about pending sex transitions.

But this is all so silly, you say, and too intrusive. No one has the right to ask those kinds of questions.

And that's precisely the point: how does anyone have the right to inquire of another's personal life, no matter how objectionable it may be to the one asking? As part of the social contract, equality has to be the overriding principle.

But religious groups counter they are being penalized for their beliefs. The decision not to engage in commerce with gays is based on the inviolate freedom of religion granted by the First Amendment.

Or maybe what we're dealing with is a matter of perspective? When a city grants a permit for the KKK to conduct a demonstration on public grounds, is the city condoning the racial hate the KKK advocates? Hardly. The city is just giving the KKK the opportunity to express itself, a right also granted by the First Amendment.

If the city is not condoning the KKK mission, why is it religious groups (not all groups, I know) see selling flowers for a gay wedding to be condoning gay marriage? There's a big difference between selling flowers and officiating at a wedding ceremony, and there's a big difference between paying an employee a clothing allowance and endorsing sex transition.

Perhaps religious groups should look to Sen. Rob Portman (R-Ohio) for guidance. He was opposed to same-sex marriage—until his college son announced he was gay. Suddenly, Portman saw things differently: "The overriding message of love and compassion that I take from the Bible, and certainly the Golden Rule, and the fact that I believe we are all created by our maker, that has all influenced me in terms of my change on this issue."

Interesting how the personal element can be so important in guiding our perspective.

We're Failing Our Children

Expelling children isn't the answer
January 25, 2014, The Columbus Dispatch

A bill has been proposed that would give Ohio schools
authority to expel, for up to 180 days, students who pose
an "imminent and severe endangerment to the health and
safety" of other students or employees. Sounds like a
good idea, doesn't it? After all, we want to make the
school environment conducive for learning. What better
way than to boot the hooligans?

While H.B. 334 may appear to have merit, the American
Academy of Pediatrics thinks the bill is a bad idea.
Why? It's reactive and does nothing to cure the problems
that underlie bad behavior. According to the AAP, the
effectiveness of expulsion "policies that demand
automatic or rigorous applications are increasingly
questionable."

H.B. 334 attempts to be fair in administering discipline.
Students who are subject to being expelled must be
given written notification of the school's intent and the
reason for expulsion, a hearing, and the right to appeal to
the school board. Due process, however, isn't the issue.

The push to increase school discipline was perhaps most
visible in 1998 when school boards were required to
adopt "a policy of zero tolerance for violent, disruptive,
or inappropriate behavior." Zero tolerance, however,
has been plagued by problems. Administrators have
failed to demonstrate critical thinking when employing
it, and its use is often discriminatory. Because it

generally lacks key elements such as fairness and flexibility, zero tolerance likely doesn't send the right message to kids.

Andrew Garner, M.D., vice president of the Ohio Chapter of the AAP, sees H.B. 334 as another step down the road of bad policy. "This bill presents the risk of adverse social, economic and health-related outcomes, and there is no evidence that suspensions and expulsions are effective deterrents to inappropriate behaviors."

Expulsion deals only with the immediacy of bad conduct, but bad conduct is often related to problems such as drug abuse, physical abuse, family problems and racial tensions. The AAP believes not enough is being done to treat these core problems and proposes several solutions.

At the top of the list is accessible early intervention for pre-school children. Challenged with the task of educating all children, public schools have to take in everyone, no matter how ill-prepared the child. According to the Annie E. Casey Foundation, 41 percent of children ages 3 to 5 in Ohio are not enrolled in nursery school, preschool or kindergarten. KidsOhio.org, reports that half of low-income youngsters in Columbus City Schools are not served by any preschool program and that these children are generally less prepared for kindergarten. KidsOhio.org maintains that rates of return are highest when kids under 5 are enrolled in good programs.

Next, the academy advocates making greater efforts to identify kids who are at-risk and provide them with assistance, such as counseling, behavior-focused study, and helping them develop problem-solving strategies.

Researchers Daniel J. Losen of UCLA and M. Karega Rausch and Shana Ritter of Indiana University have found that proactive intervention, building connections with students, and creating better options for more serious infractions are the common foundations among successful schools. In the words of a principal interviewed by the researchers, "If you can create a culture where kids feel respected and safe and secure, then we can get to the nuts and bolts of teaching."

The third idea is to promote school-wide support for positive behavior where "desired behaviors are actively taught, clearly and consistently expected, and positively recognized and acknowledged." As this program is practiced, problems decrease.

"Research suggests that students who experience suspension and expulsion are ten times more likely to drop out of school," stated Garner. Dealing with troubled students isn't just a matter of altruism but an issue that affects revenue and expense.

A 2009 Northeastern University study showed that, in comparison to high school graduates, dropouts had an employment rate in 2007 that was 22 percentage points lower; they earned $6,000 less annually. Translation: less tax revenue.

PBS reported in March 2013 that 68 percent of all males in federal and state prisons do not have high school diplomas. As suspensions and expulsions increase, incarceration rates increase—giving rise to the phrase, "school to prison pipeline"—which means more government expense.

Getting rid of the troublemakers is expedient and politically attractive, but it doesn't solve the underlying problems. Either we invest resources to address those problems now, or we expel more kids and deal with the financial consequences later.

Foster kids need help as they age out of system
April 23, 2018, The Columbus Dispatch

Imagine being in the foster care system for years and, suddenly, on your 18th birthday, you're expected to fend for yourself. Get a job, find a place to live and make good of yourself. It's a tall order for any 18-year-old, all the more so when you've suffered abuse or neglect or drug dependency has been part of your world.

The odds are stacked against this group. Based on research by Ohio Fostering Connections, a coalition that advocates for foster youth, by the time these teens reach age 21 more than 20% will experience homelessness, 71% of women will be pregnant, only 36% will be working either full or part time, and 36% will have been incarcerated. Nearly half will lack a high school degree or GED.

Worse yet, they're especially vulnerable to human trafficking. The National Youth Foster Institute reports that 60% of all child sex trafficking victims have been in the child welfare system.

Provide these 18-year-olds with extended assistance, however, and good things happen. School enrollment and high school graduation/GED rates increase, and homelessness and incarceration rates decrease.

The Ohio General Assembly addressed the problem in 2016 by passing the Fostering Connections Act, which authorized the Department of Jobs and Family Services

(ODJFS) to implement a new service program known as "Bridges." Now, those who age out of foster care are eligible for continued services until age 21.

ODJFS contracted with the Child and Family Health Collaborative to administer Bridges state-wide. The goal is to help these teens live independently. Financial assistance for room and board is available, as is coaching from social workers who help their clients create and achieve educational and employment goals and teach critical thinking, financial management and self-care.

Marc Mecum oversees the Collaborative and emphasis that Bridges is not an extension of foster care. "These are young adults we're guiding. There's no hand holding here. We want to empower these people and give them the tools to be successful."

MeCum says that only 25 other states provide extended services for foster care youths. Ohio's is the only state with a program administered by a non-profit.

Too new to evaluate fully, shortcoming in the program are apparent, says Lisa Brooks of Sojouners Care Network, a non-profit serving southeastern Ohio as a Bridges provider. For one, eligibility criteria—be enrolled in school or employed for 80 hours a month or be medically exempted from either—is a hurdle for many. So too is the date of emancipation. A candidate must have emancipated from foster care at age 18; no matter how many housing transitions a teen may have had, if he left the system at 17, he's ineligible.

In addition, the paperwork is tough. "The eligibility documentation is detail-driven and difficult to obtain." says Brooks. "It's hardly an easy process."

Adding to the problem is that foster care youth don't get adequate life-skills training. While always mandated, "there has been inconsistency in the state in how it's administered," says Marcus Games, Sojouners' co-executive director. "Some counties were good; others not so good."

The problem has been remedied in part by the new Comprehensive Case Management and Employment Program, which is funded with federal dollars and administered by ODJFS. CCMEP brings together teachers, case workers and other specialists to help prepare foster youth 14 years and older for the work force. "Finally," said Games, "we're seeing a coordinated effort in the state."

The challenges these young adults face is largely based, according to Games, "on the absence of permanent relationships in their lives—sources of support they can fall back on." Without the stability that comes from permanent relationships, these young adults are adrift, trying to make do with systems provided by the state.

Ohio is making headway, but it's still a scary proposition for an 18-year-old who ages out of the system.

Boost child support payments by helping parents
June 23, 2020, The Columbus Dispatch

London Chapman owes over $200,000 in child support and has fathered 13 children by nine women. What to do?

In a criminal proceeding, a court in Lorain County ordered Chapman to "make all reasonable efforts to avoid impregnating a woman" until he can prove he is able to support the children he already has. An appellate court agreed. The Ohio Supreme Court is about to weigh in.

The trial court's order seems to make sense. If you can't support 13 children, why should you be fathering more? But, like many things, it's more complicated than that.

The right to procreate has long been considered a fundamental right protected by the U.S. Constitution. In 1942, the U.S. Supreme Court addressed an Oklahoma law that mandated sterilization for offenders who were convicted of two or more felonies of "mortal turpitude." The felonies in that case consisted of stealing chickens and two counts of armed robbery.

Recognizing a basic civil right was at issue—"Marriage and procreation are fundamental to the very existence and survival of the race"—the court was bothered by the law's inequal application. Fraud constituted moral turpitude under the law, but embezzlement didn't. With no justification for its unequal application, the law was struck down.

Just 15 years earlier when reviewing a Virginia law that permitted sterilizing the "feeble minded," the court voiced a different attitude. The state wanted to sterilize a pregnant 17-year old girl, who had already given birth once. Both she and her mother were confined at an institution because of their "feeble-mindedness."

The law was upheld in a cringeworthy opinion written by Justice Oliver Wendell Holmes. "It is better for all the world if ... society can prevent those who are manifestly unfit from continuing their kind. . . . Three generations of imbeciles are enough."

The state of Ohio must convince the Ohio Supreme Court that ordering Chapman not to procreate—a fundamental right—is "supported by sufficiently important state interests" and is "closely tailored to effectuate only those interests," the standard articulated by the U.S. Supreme Court in 1978.

How does banning Chapman from fathering children ensure that he supports the children he has or prevent him from incurring other financial obligations? His crime—failing to meet his financial obligations—is only tangentially related to having children in the future.

Plus, there's the uncomfortable issue of enforcement. Must Chapman abstain from sex? Does birth control constitute compliance? What kind?

Let's put Chapman's case in perspective. It's extreme and significant only because of the constitutional issue it presents. There may be no good way of dealing with Chapman at this point. The time for getting him on track passed years back.

Still, compliance for more typical cases is a problem. About 100 or so child support cases are on the criminal docket in Lorain County court every other week.

Generational poverty likely plays a role. According to Franklin County's Child Support Enforcement Agency, many non-paying parents earn less than $10,000 a year and are struggling. They may have the desire but not the ability to meet their obligations.

Courts may be effective in dealing with parents who can, but choose not to pay, but aren't equipped to deal with parents who have little means and stymied by obstacles. For this group, a court in Franklin County created in 2014 a diversion program called Compass.

Compass provides employment assistance, parenting classes and access to community service providers to help parents overcome the obstacles—a felony conviction is often a barrier to employment—that prevent them from meeting their obligations. The program generally results in better outcomes and at less expense than the court system.

As of last count, two other courts in Ohio have similar programs, and some 25 county child support agencies engage in collaborative programs with other agencies. Want to improve compliance? Follow the lead of these courts and agencies and provide more mentoring and navigating for parents who lack the wherewithal to overcome the obstacles they face.

About the author

I'm a business lawyer and litigator with The Behal Law Group in Columbus, Ohio. My wife, Debbie, and I have four children, four grandchildren, and a dog named Sam.

When I'm not practicing law, I write op-eds for The Columbus Dispatch, publish my blog, Consider This by JD, and lend a hand to Ohioans to Stop Executions, Dad2B and Embark (a prison ministry).

My law partner, John Gonzales (one of the best trial lawyers in Columbus), and I produce a podcast, Lawyer Up! Columbus, where we discuss with our guests a variety of legal and social justice issues. You can find our podcast at www.lawyerupcolumbus.com and our law firm at www.behallaw.com.

You can reach me at jdaurora@behallaw.com.

www.ingramcontent.com/pod-product-compliance
Lightning Source LLC
Chambersburg PA
CBHW070652250726
48662CB00001B/84